Current Thought on Curriculum

1985 ASCD Yearbook

Association for Supervision
and Curriculum Development
225 North Washington Street
Alexandria, VA 22314

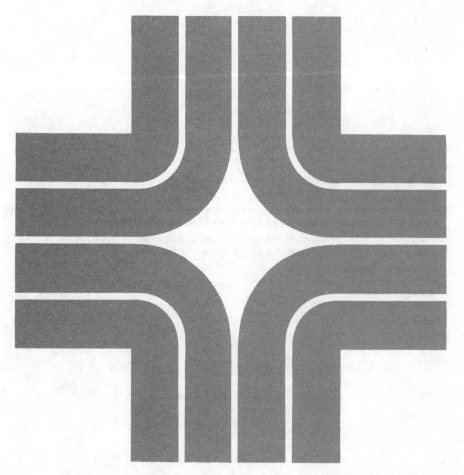

Dedicated to James B. Macdonald

ASCD stock number: 610-84358
ISBN: 0-87120-129-1
Library of Congress
  Card Catalog No.: 85-070039

Price: $12.00

Contents

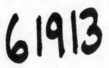

Acknowledgements

I would like to acknowledge the contributions of two groups of people who helped to make this volume possible: the contributing authors and my colleagues during the 1983-84 academic year at Fernuniversität, Hagen, West Germany.

Editing a book is made more or less difficult and more or less rewarding largely through the efforts of the contributing authors. The authors of *Current Thought on Curriculum* definitely made my job easier. I received copy on time, and I was able to make editorial suggestions without fear of bruising anyone's ego. The contributions were substantively excellent and I learned a good deal from the extensive editorial give and take.

I was, during the 1983-84 academic year, a guest professor in the department Theorie der Schule und des Unterrichts (roughly Curriculum and Instruction) at Fernuniversität in Hagen, West Germany. During that year, one of my principal tasks was to write a course on the U.S. school system for Fernuniversität students. That work served as the basis of my contribution to this volume. As I wrote the course, I was greatly assisted by the comments, suggestions, and criticisms of my colleagues in Theorie der Schule und des Unterrichts. They pushed and poked at my assumptions and demanded clarification for my sometimes vague formulations. They helped me learn to see the U.S. educational system as an outsider might view it—a useful perspective for an academic to cultivate.

My colleagues in Hagen were Isle Bange, Klaus-Dieter Eubel, Klaus Hage, Erda Milbradt, Heinz-Jörg Oehlschläger, and Dieter Schwittmann. They were the sort of colleagues an academic hopes for. A good deal of what may be worthy in my chapter is the result of my contact with them.

Alex Molnar
Milwaukee, 1985

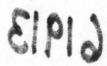

Foreword

T hose of us who operate schools sometimes wonder about the usefulness of those who observe and analyze them. We take the professors' graduate classes because, if we want new certificates, we must—but also because the classes can be intellectually stimulating.

The gap between educational town and gown has widened in recent years until, as Gail McCutcheon writes in this volume, it has become a Grand Canyon. Practitioners and professors of curriculum are members of two foreign cultures who visit each other's territory once in awhile, but who feel more comfortable with their own kind. The trend is reflected in ASCD where, for example, fewer professors are members of governance groups than they once were.

This yearbook is an effort to counteract that trend. Some of the leading curriculum theorists were asked to convey their ideas and those of their colleagues regarding key issues facing educators in the 1980s. Some of these issues, such as those discussed by Decker Walker in his chapter on technology, 1ve emerged only recently. Others, because they are inherent in the very nature of education, are perennial.

Are these reflections relevant to those of us "on the firing line?" If they are not, we are condemned to grope pragmatically for whatever seems most expedient at the time, because most of us have too few opportunities to view our day-to-day actions from a broader perspective. We need to think deeply about the meaning and direction of our incremental decisions. This book offers that opportunity.

PHIL C. ROBINSON
ASCD President, 1984-85

Introduction

ALEX MOLNAR

The 1985 ASCD yearbook is an invitation for practitioners and scholars to talk about current issues and continuing concerns. The contributors to this volume recognize that academics and practitioners need to share each other's knowledge, skill, and experience.

To a great extent, academics and educational practitioners live in different worlds, respond to different pressures, and must satisfy different audiences. None of this is likely to change anytime soon. Nevertheless, academics and practitioners need each other because each occupies a territory necessary for the other to explore if they are to be effective in their work.

At present the relationship between academics and practitioners is analogous to the relationship between two players in the game of "Prisoner's Dilemma," described by Axelrod as follows:

> In the Prisoner's Dilemma game, there are two players. Each has two choices, namely cooperate or defect. Each must make the choice without knowing what the other will do. No matter what the other does, defection yields a higher payoff than cooperation. The dilemma is that if both defect, they do worse than if both had cooperated. . . .
>
> The way the game works is shown in Figure 1. One player chooses a row, either cooperating or defecting. The other player simultaneously chooses a column, either cooperating or defecting. Together, these choices result in one of the four possible outcomes shown in the matrix. If both players cooperate, both do fairly well. Both get R, the *reward for mutual cooperation*. In the concrete illustration of Figure 1, the reward is three points. This number might, for example, be a payoff in dollars that each player gets for that outcome. If one

FIGURE 1
The Prisoner's Dilemma

		Column Player	
		Cooperate	*Defect*
Row Player	Cooperate	$R = 3, R = 3$ Reward for mutual cooperation	$S = O, T = 5$ Sucker's payoff, and temptation to defect
	Defect	$T = 5, S = 0$ Temptation to defect and sucker's payoff	$P = 1, P = 1$ Punishment for mutual defection

NOTE: The payoffs to the row-chooser are listed first.

player cooperates but the other defects, the defecting player gets the *temptation to defect*, while the cooperating player gets the *sucker's payoff*. In the example, these are five points and zero points respectively. If both defect, both get one point, the *punishment for mutual defection*. . . .

The Prisoner's Dilemma is simply an abstract formulation of some very common and very interesting situations in which what is best for each person individually leads to mutual defection, whereas everyone would have been better off with mutual cooperation.[1]

Academics and practitioners have been, to use Axelrod's words, mutually defecting for years, for very good reasons, and with painful consequences. Scholars are asked to be relevant to, but are rarely expected to learn from, practitioners. Practitioners are told to value the theories of academics, but they rarely offered help in identifying and thinking about how their own theories shape and direct the decisions they make. Nor is much help offered in looking at how the theories that actually guide a professional's practice are developed and how they can be refined.

The fact that academics and practitioners are rewarded for different behaviors does not explain the mutual irrelevance of academics and practitioners in each other's daily affairs. There are other factors at work. Perhaps principal among them are two beliefs: that professional education is structured as a top–down hierarchy with academics at the top and classroom teachers at the bottom; and that academics and practitioners must do work that is mutually relevant if it is to be useful. Academics who work in schools of education and who say that their work does not have to do with schools, and teachers who roll their eyes at the mention of the word "theory" and whose conception of professional training doesn't go beyond learning how to use the teacher's guide for the new reading program, to some extent reflect the same problem—the gulf between academics and practitioners.

Rather than uncritically defining relevance as a solution, academics and practitioners might do better to define their relationship by asking, "Even though our work is different, what can we learn from each other?" When Rogers, for example, discusses qualitative and aesthetic views of the curriculum, he describes clearly how badly academics need the living reality of schools and classrooms to organize their thinking and to *develop* their theories—not just test them. When McCutcheon and Wolfson examine the reality of the personal theories that practitioners develop, they are explaining how academics can do something other than teach practitioners their theories. They are suggesting that academics can help practitioners clarify and develop their own theories. In these instances, neither academics nor practitioners need give up their own goals and interests. The point is that educators can learn how to cooperate to help each other reach *different* goals.

It is my hope that this yearbook will be *used* to foster that kind of cooperation. Each of the chapters maps out a territory that can be explored by groups of scholars and practitioners in a variety of professional forums.

In "Schools and Their Curriculum: A Continuing Controversy," I take up the question: why are schools and their curriculums so often involved in public controversy? I point out that the role and function of public education in the United States is controversial, in part, because the structure of public education, as it has developed in the United States, makes controversy inevitable. The question as to whether this or that controversy is good or bad for public education is a matter to be resolved in individual instances. However, for practitioners who are caught up in a controversy, there may be both comfort and guidance in being able to understand the tensions built into public education in the U.S. Those tensions are both substantive ("Who determines what will be taught to ten-year-olds in this district?") and structural ("What is the meaning of local control in relation to an issue like standardized testing?"). If controversy is inherent in the way public education in the U.S. is structured, then it will do no good for practitioners to hope it will go away. It will not. Controversy will occur again and again. Accepting that reality and attempting to understand the framework within which the controversy plays itself out may help practitioners work more constructively with the inevitable controversy when it arises.

One often-repeated complaint of experienced practitioners is the seemingly cyclical nature of educational reform. It has often been said that public education is beset by fads. Everything seems constantly to be changing, yet nothing fundamental seems to change. The role of professional educators in contributing to this problem is arguable. What seems less arguable is the essential truth of the observation. In his chapter, "Three Currents of American Curriculum Thought," Kliebard helps us to understand the historical reality underlying this truth. He helps make it possible to understand curricular change as something other than merely capricious. There were and are people struggling in a web of historical circumstance who have attempted to shape and direct the nature of public schooling. There is a certain comfort in knowing that although curricular change often *appears* to be mysterious and random, it is not. At least not entirely. Even the "rapid change/no real change" contradiction, which has had teachers, professors, principals, and other interested observers perennially scratching their heads, can itself be more clearly understood by studying the structure and historical development of schools and school curriculum.

It is reasonable to suggest that when practitioners are caught up in difficulties, they rarely expect to find help in scholarly literature. This is the problem McCutcheon analyzes in "Curriculum Theory/Curriculum Practice: A Gap or The Grand Canyon?" McCutcheon takes a look at what has created the "Grand Canyon" between scholars and practitioners and what can be done to bridge it. She argues that practitioners and scholars each possess knowledge vital to the other. In making her point, McCutcheon draws a distinction between "personal theories of action" and "generic theories," the former being the domain of the practitioner, the latter of the scholar.

In some ways the distinction McCutcheon makes between personal theories of action and generic theory helps to clarify why Wolfson can argue in "Psychological Theory and Curricular Thinking" that the psychological theories of academics are only tenuously connected to curriculum decision making. Wolfson examines how various psychological theories influence the people who make curriculum decisions, whether they make them as professionals working for textbook firms, state departments of public instruction, or individual school districts. Wolfson asks us to consider how those "commonsensical" beliefs that educators hold about the psychology of children come to be "common sense." Her approach asks us to consider that the psychology that finds its way into our schools is to a significant extent a function of the psychology of curriculum makers. Wolfson's psychology is not, however, a psychology of isolated individuals, because she acknowledges the significance of social and cultural context in shaping one's psychological orientation and one's being. Therefore, every decision of a curriculum maker who seeks to apply psychological principles in organizing school curriculum is at once a personal, a social, and a political decision.

It is interesting to compare Apple's chapter to his contribution in the 1977 volume *Curriculum Theory*.[2] In a chapter he co-authored with Nancy King, "What do Schools Teach?" Apple explored the nature of what he described as the "hidden curriculum." His chapter in this volume, "Making Knowledge Legitimate: Power, Profit, and The Textbook," examines that most visible part of the school curriculum, the textbook. Apple wants to look more closely at how what gets taught is determined by the textbook industry. Although his work is, by his own admission, in its early stages, Apple presents us with a good case for looking more closely at the politics and sociology of the textbook industry. For the practitioner this work is of potentially enormous importance insofar as it can help practitioners become more critical consumers of commercially produced text materials. The work also exposes for the practitioner a new aspect of an old struggle in American education: the nature and meaning of local control.

In "Curriculum and Technology," Walker outlines some of the thinking that has recently given his work a new direction. Over the past several years, experience with computers has rapidly become one of the standard elements of elementary and secondary school curriculums. Walker is interested in computers and their potential for transforming the nature of school curriculums and perhaps even the organization and meaning of public education itself. However, he cautions that the spread of computer usage in public schools is only one highly visible part of a broader relationship, that of the schools to technology and to technological change. Can or should schools as they are currently organized transform themselves enough to make meaningful use of a powerful new technology such as computers? Can or should computers fit in and serve existing curricular arrangements? How will or could schools transform and be transformed by emerging technologies? These are some of the questions Walker asks us to consider and wrestle with. While he provides no definite answers (there are none), he does help in formulating some of the more important questions.

"Qualitative and Aesthetic Views of Curriculum and Curriculum Making" is Rogers' review of approaches to assessing school curriculums using qualitative rather than quantitative criteria. Although the shortcomings of quantitative measures in curriculum evaluation have been frequently discussed over the last several years, there can be little doubt that most curricular assessment is conducted in quantitative rather than qualitative terms. In fact, a good deal of what is currently referred to as curriculum evaluation is principally the tabulation of student performance on standardized tests. Rogers argues that professional educators should and can do differently. Rogers not only makes the case for qualitative assessment, he goes further and offers concrete suggestions for practitioners who feel that the quantitative measures they are currently using are not adequate.

In perhaps the most theoretical chapter in the book, "Education and Schooling: Curriculum From a Global Perspective," Lundgren challenges the reader to see education as a science and to understand what educational science might contribute to human knowledge. To call Lundgren's contribution theoretical is not to damn it as useless to the practitioner. Lundgren's chapter is the last in the book for good reason. After reading the first seven chapters, readers are invited to use the concepts Lundgren outlines to sharpen their understanding of the other contributions. Here is theory used as it should be used, to sharpen and clarify rather than obscure and confuse. Lundgren's chapter is challenging reading, but ultimately worth the effort to scholar and practitioner alike.

It is the hope of the contributors to this book that it will be used in a variety of professional forums, such as school inservice sessions, college courses, and symposia at professional meetings to help academics and practitioners move away from mutual "defection" and move toward mutual cooperation. If the 1985 ASCD Yearbook contributes in some small way to this movement, it will have been an enormous success.

Notes

[1] Robert Axelrod, *The Evolution of Cooperation* (New York: Basic Books, 1984), pp. 6-9.
[2] Michael Apple and Nancy King, "What Do Schools Teach?" in *Curriculum Theory*, eds. A. Molnar and J. A. Zahorik (Washington, D.C.: Association for Supervision and Curriculum Development, 1977), pp. 108-126.

Chapter 1.
Schools and Their Curriculum:
A Continuing Controversy

ALEX MOLNAR

Controversy is not new to U.S. schools. It's been with them for a long time. In fact, the U.S. school system is, in many respects, a child of social and political controversy and struggle.

Following the Revolution, Americans (or, perhaps more accurately, many of the leading political figures of the time) identified and expressed an important role for education in the new republic. To a large extent they advocated a state-supported public school system as a safeguard against the possibility of either the creation of an American aristocracy or, with an eye toward France, the degeneration of the republic into mob rule. Such schools were to be the mechanism by which the new republic was to reconcile the apparent contradiction between the necessity for public order and the existence of a political democracy. This argument was advanced again and again throughout the 19th century and into the 20th century. Benjamin Rush, a republican theorist, wrote as early as 1786:

> Most of the distresses of our country, and of the mistakes which Europeans have formed of us, have arisen from a belief that the American revolution is over. This is so far from being the case that we have only finished the first act of a great drama. We have changed our forms of government, but it remains yet to effect a revolution in our principles, opinions, and manners so as to accom-

Alex Molnar is Associate Professor, Department of Curriculum and Instruction, University of Wisconsin-Milwaukee.

modate them to the forms of government we have adopted. This is the most difficult part of the business of the patriots and legislatures of our country.[1]

Kaestle quotes what is perhaps the most famous line from Rush in his book, *Pillars of the Republic:*

> I consider it as possible to convert men into republican machines. This must be done if we expect them to perform their parts properly in the great machine of state.[2]

Although Rush's language was more flamboyant than most, there is little doubt that the significance such republican theorists gave the idea that children had to learn the ideological prerequisites for citizenship provided an important intellectual motive force behind the drive for tax-supported common schools increasingly controlled and regulated by the state.

During the colonial period, at least a basic level of educational attainment was widely accomplished—primarily through informal, local neighborhood initiatives. Each locality controlled its own schools and funded them in ways that it deemed appropriate. Most often the schools were financed by direct contributions from parents themselves or from the church or, in the instance of children too poor to pay to go to school, charity schools were sometimes provided. However, nowhere in the colonies was public education required by law nor school attendance compulsory; nor were schools entirely, or even primarily, supported by tax money.[3]

To many Americans of the early national period, the idea that the state should in any way regulate and control what their children would be taught was undemocratic and a threat to religious freedom, local political authority, and ethnic identity. Questions such as who should control the schools, whether teaching was a profession, how schools should be financed, and the desired degree of standardization among the schools were all hotly debated throughout most of the 19th century. To a certain extent, it would be fair to say that the debate over public education in the U.S., begun in the 19th century and continuing today, is a debate over competing visions of U.S. society.

The U.S. of the early 19th century was primarily a rural nation of tradesmen, small farmers, and businessmen. Thomas Jefferson's ideal of the American citizen was drawn from the small farmers and the yeomen of his day, who were viewed as possessing the necessary virtues of being both participants in a democracy and God-fearing Christians. They were independent, self-sufficient, thrifty, and perhaps most important, in control of their own affairs. Given this setting it is hardly surprising that many citizens were quite content with the system of education they had inherited from the colonial period; a system, it was argued, that provided at least a rudimentary education on a scale unknown in any other contemporary society. It offered flexibility in which each locality could determine what would be taught, hire the teacher to teach it, determine the appropriate facility, and finance the school in ways that they thought proper. (It was not uncommon, for example, for teachers in rural schools to be paid in produce instead of money.) Another important issue in many localities was the right of children to be taught in the language of their parents, which was sometimes not English. This was a right that German parents in particular struggled long and hard to protect. To this day the one-room, locally controlled schoolhouse still represents, for many Americans, a democratic ideal in which the diversity of education provided in different localities reflects the diversity of the U.S. itself.

Against this democratic ideal republican political and educational theorists, such as Horace Mann in Massachusetts, continued to argue that a state-supported common school system was essential if American students were to learn the values necessary for effective citizenship. The republicans also maintained that children of all classes should go to school together. As the U.S. became increasingly urban (a trend of growing significance in the 19th century) republicans argued that the country was threatened by a large, uneducated working class and that the education of this class was essential to the preservation of a republican form of government.

The concept of equality of opportunity was advanced in support of the proposition that common schools would be the principle mechanism for assuring the orderly progress of the new republic. deLone points out that during the 1820s and 1830s, Thomas Jefferson's idea of equal opportunity was accepted by both the democratic and the traditionally conservative Whig parties as a cornerstone of their social thinking.[4] The idea was relatively straight forward: children, regardless of the class into which they were born, would be given an equal opportunity to compete for the goods that society had to offer. It was argued that since America was not, in the European sense, a rigid class-based society with a hereditary aristocracy, the concept of equality of opportunity had a good deal to commend it. It would help assure that U.S. society would be shaped by talent rather than privilege. The concept of equality of opportunity also fit comfortably with the prevalent Protestant religious ideology and its ethic of hard work and thriftiness. If a child of humble origins, so it was said, was intelligent and applied himself, and was thrifty and persevering, he could make a success of himself. Equality of opportunity was the fuel and schools were to be the engine that would make it possible for such children to compete with others whose birth had placed them at a relative advantage. Once equality of opportunity in a democratic society was accepted as a goal of American social policy, the push for a state-supported common school as its programmatic expression seemed like good common sense.

The vision of a state-supported common school system was not a plan for the radical transformation of society along egalitarian lines; quite the contrary, it was a blueprint for preserving the stability and continuity of republican society without too much social upheaval. No one says it more clearly than Horace Mann, who is regarded by many as one of the principal architects of the modern American public school system. Mann, the first secretary of the Massachusetts Board of Education, argued in his 12th annual report to the state Board of Education in 1848 (a year in which much of Europe was in open revolt and in which the Communist Manifesto was published):

> Education, then, beyond all other devices of human origin, is the great equalizer of the conditions of men—the balance wheel of the social machinery. . . . It does better than to disarm the poor of their hostility toward the rich; it prevents being poor.[5]

An ideological counterpoint to Mann and the concept of equality of opportunity and advancement in society through achievement in school was provided by Orestes Brownson, who struggled unsuccessfully in Massachusetts to dismantle the Board of Education and to eliminate Mann's position. Brownson argued:

> We regard the improvement of the adult as a means of advancing the child rather than the education of the child as the means of advancing the adult.[6]

Such were the battle lines in the fight for the common school during the 19th century.

Evolution of State Control of Education

Although there was enormous controversy over the proper scope and form of public education as well as the state's role, if any, in providing it, there is little reason to doubt that education was valued by Americans in the early 19th century. This is demonstrated by the number of private schools that sprung up in the cities and in the large number of small schools serving rural neighborhood districts. A state-supported common school system was controversial because many citizens felt a deep conviction that local control was essential in a democracy, had a commitment to individual choice, and believed that the existing educational arrangements were adequate to meet the needs of their communities and the country. Although the common school reformers eventually prevailed, it would be inaccurate to characterize the debate over the establishment of a state-supported common school system as waged between pro- and anti-education forces. In fact, it might be argued that the common school reformers carried the day less because of their ideological correctness than because the trend toward the urbanization of American society worked in their favor.

Katz uses the New York Public School Society, founded in 1805 as the New York Free School Society dedicated to "extending the means of education to such poor children as do not belong to, or are not provided for by, any religious society," as an example of the evolution of state control over the public systems in American cities.[7] The New York Free School Society took as its task to provide education for those children whose parents were too poor to provide for them otherwise and who for some reason were not eligible to be educated in any of the number of church-supported schools in the city. The New York Free School Society was directed and administered by a volunteer group drawn largely from the upper strata of New York society who tended to see their work as a public responsibility. At first the society's aim was relatively straightforward and not especially conflictual: to provide a minimal level of education to the "unchurched" poor, a task for which the society received money from the state as well as from private donations. However, Katz reports that by 1825 when the New York *Free* School Society renamed itself the New York *Public* School Society, it was arguing that no church-supported school should receive public tax money. The Society, he says, held that the goals of education would be best served by the establishment of a single nonsectarian school system. Needless to say, the Society saw itself as the agency to guide and direct such a system. The New York state legislature apparently agreed, and the New York Public School Society was given authority to disperse virtually all of the public money appropriated for elementary education in the city of New York.

Such voluntary societies (invariably dominated by a wealthy elite) came under increasing criticism in the 19th century as an inappropriate mechanism to administer public educational funds. The criticisms were leveled by different groups and for different reasons. Immigrant groups, Catholics primarily, feared the imposition of a common educational format on populations of students whom they regarded as quite different from one another. Furthermore, they argued that control and direction of educational policy by volunteer organizations cut off any possibility for meaningful parental and local political control over the schools. Instead, they often proposed the rural model, that each neighborhood should be able to hire and fire teachers, select curriculums, and provide a school facility for the children of the neighborhood as the appropriate model for urban education. Proponents contended that this would assure the responsiveness of the schools.

Republican school reformers, on the other hand, wanted *neither* schools controlled by voluntary organizations, dominated by an elite group, nor did they want complete authority over schools to reside in individual localities. Further, they wanted to disassociate the idea of a free *public* school from the idea of a free *charity* school. They argued that education was an important state responsibility and therefore advocated state boards of education headed by a secretary of education to oversee policy, free public schools supported completely by taxes, elected central boards of education, and normal schools for the preparation of teachers.

Although it was the republican common school crusaders who fought for free common education for all children that eventually carried the day in the 19th century, the evolution of the New York Free School Society provides an example of how long the process took. The decision of the Society in 1825 to change its name and invite non-indigent children to attend was, according to Kaestle, a critical step in the transition of New York schools from a charity to a common school system. However, it was not until 1853 that the system became entirely public, no longer supported by private benevolence as well as public grants and not run by a self-perpetuating board of trustees. It was, Kaestle writes, several more decades before the New York common schools lost their stigma as charity schools.[8]

The Advent of the Public High School

It should not be surprising that as the common school debate advanced in the 19th century, free public high schools would be proposed as the logical extension of free publicly supported common schools. When the first public high school was opened in Boston, Massachusetts, in 1821, private academies dominated secondary education.

According to Tyack, the 19th century public high school was primarily an urban phenomenon.[9] Just what the high school was supposed to be and whom it was supposed to serve seems to have been a matter of confusion and controversy since the first high school was established. Tyack quotes one educator as saying in 1892:

> The term high school is the vaguest in the school vocabulary. It covers an endless variety of schools with an infinite variety of courses of study, aims, ideals, and methods.[10]

The quote sounds remarkably similar in tone to Tanner, writing in 1984:

> ... unless the profession sorts out the contradictory prescriptions for reform, schools will continue to be buffeted by conflicting demands and will ride whatever sociopolitical tide is dominant.[11]

The high school eventually replaced the academy. In many communities the local academy was regarded as a public institution because it provided a public service in educating the young of the community. As the public high school gradually gained ascendency over the academy, some academies became elementary schools, others became colleges. Some associated themselves with a church, and still others were transformed into public high schools.

Academies came under increasing pressure from school reformers in the 19th century, because as Katz has written:

> Academies represented the quintessence of volunteerism as noblesse oblige because they rapidly diffused throughout the country a combination of public goals and private control wrapped in the mantle of disinterested service. But the emergence of a new definition of "public school" signaled the demise of corporate volunteerism as public policy. George Boutwell, onetime governor of Massachusetts, secretary of the board of education, and eventually U.S. Senator, stated the matter with precision: "A public school I understand to be a school established by the public supported chiefly or entirely by the public, controlled by the public, and accessible to the public upon terms of equality without special charge for tuition . . . Although they [academies] were sometimes, upon a super-ficial view, supposed to be public, schools of that sort were only public in their use, but not in their foundation or control, and are therefore not public schools."[12]

It was during the period from about 1890 to about 1940, when countless political battles were fought over control of urban school systems, that the high school assumed its contemporary form as a mass institution.

In the late 19th century, city schools were typically controlled by large school boards whose membership sometimes exceeded 20 members. In addition to a central school board, there were often many smaller so-called ward boards which exercised a good deal of control over education in their locality. Administrative and political control of the schools during this period was diffuse, contentious, and often corrupt.

Centralizing Control of Education

It is important to keep in mind that the urbanization of the U.S. did not occur by magic. It was principally the result of industrialization. By the late 19th century industrialization had helped give rise to the development of a professional and corporate managerial class. It was this class (which included university professors and school managers) that helped provide the motive force behind centralizing control of American public schools in the hands of "nonpolitical" school boards which would set policy but which would leave the management and administration of the system in the hands of education "experts." The late 19th and early 20th century was a time of considerable faith in "scientific" principles of all sorts, including the principles of "scientific management" as applied in industry. Not surprisingly the model for a school board according to these reformers, was a corporate board of directors. Efforts to centralize the power of the school board were successful. As Tyack reports:

> In 1893 in the 28 cities having populations of 100,000 or more, there were 603 central school board members—an average of 21.5 per city; in addition, there were hundreds of ward board members in some of the larger cities. By 1913, the number of central school board members in those cities had been dropped to 264, or an average of about 10.2, while the ward boards had all but disappeared and most central board members were elected at large. By 1923 the numbers had continued to diminish until the median was seven members.[13]

The school reformers of the late 19th and early 20th century who argued for centralized control over schools continued in a long line of republican reformers who hoped to create an orderly state-supported public school system. They were concerned that a decentralized school system not regulated by the state would be incapable of producing a citizenry capable of preserving the republic. These reformers played on the same theme as those of the early national period when they described a need to "Americanize" the millions of newly arrived immigrant children. As the republican common school reformers before them, they saw the public school system as the social mechanism necessary to produce a loyal citizenry.

Beginning during the late 19th century the high school evolved from an institution which served a relatively small number of students drawn primarily from the middle ranks of American society to one which the great majority of American children attend for at least a time. In 1890, American high schools enrolled approximately 360,000; 70 years later they enrolled 83.2 percent of all 14 to 17-year-olds.[14]

Professional Influences

The corporate and professional elite that took increasing control over city school systems during the late 19th and early 20th century also took the lead in defining a number of problems faced by those schools. For example, as high school enrollment grew, lack of standard college admission procedures was seen as a problem. Colleges drew students from all across the country. Often these students had highly varied educational preparation. In part in response to this perceived problem, accrediting associations, professional organizations that set and control standards of their member institutions, were established. The College Entrance Examination, the first test designed to measure the aptitude of applicants, was designed and administered for the first time in 1901. Arguably the most far-reaching attempt to set a standard for high schools was the report of the "Committee of Ten" of the National Education Association (NEA).[15] Appointed in 1892, the "Committee of Ten" took as its task nothing less than to recommend the selection and organization of high school curriculum.

A second influential NEA report, *Cardinal Principles of Secondary Education*,[16] issued in 1918, reflected the American educational progressivism of the period and called for a curriculum based on a scientific assessment of individual and social needs. Although these two reports are quite different, they are good examples of how professional recommendations reflected and influenced the nature of secondary education during this important period. These reports were followed by a third National Education Association study entitled *Education for ALL American Youth*,[17] issued during World War II, which may well have represented a high-water mark for the influence of progressive ideas in American education.

By the late 1940s and early 1950s progressive curriculum ideas had come under increasing attack. With the launching of the first satellite by the Soviet Union, the curriculum field was under irresistible pressure from within and without to return to intellectual training and the disciplines. Books such as Jerome Bruner's *The Process of Education*,[18] in which Bruner argues that academic disciplines have an inherent structure that can be taught meaningfully at virtually every grade level, and yet another statement by the National Education Association entitled, *The Central Purpose of American Education*,[19] which emphasized the importance of intellectual training as the purpose of American secondary education, are two indications of how the trend away from progressive ideas was reflected in the professional literature.

The series of NEA reports beginning with the report of the "Committee of Ten," the writing of educational scholars such as John Dewey,[20] George Counts,[21] and Jerome Bruner,[22] and educational critics such as H. G. Rickover,[23] on through the work of James Coleman[24] and Charles Silverman[25] illustrate how throughout the late 19th and 20th centuries professional organizations, educational scholars and critics, private foundations, and the government have responded to and attempted to shape social trends bearing on pubic education. The latest spate of reports (perhaps the most widely publicized among them being *A Nation At Risk*), illustrate that perceived social problems continue to be translated into educational problems,[26] a phenomenon that helps assure a controversial future for public education in the U.S.

It is not only the social *function* of public schooling or the *general* direction (progressive vs. traditional principles) of curriculums that are controversial. What, if any, controversial social topics should find their way into professional discourse and school curriculums is also a matter of continuing professional and public debate. This is not a mysterious circumstance when one considers that schools are by and large expected to educate students about the *formal* aspects of U.S. republican democracy while to a great extent (at least in practice) steering clear of the substantive (and often controversial) issues that are fought over within that framework.

Among the recent examples of continuing professional recognition of and response to social issues and problems are the resolutions on critical contemporary issues and on a nuclear freeze adopted by the Association for Supervision and Curriculum Development (ASCD). The ASCD Board of Directors on March 22, 1982, approved the following resolution:

> Issues such as nuclear disarmament, environmental protection, population growth, world hunger, and human rights concern every inhabitant of our planet. Each of us is responsible individually for expressing concern and for being active in assuring that our global future is desirable. ASCD also has a responsibility as an organization to express the beliefs and concerns of the membership and to support members' rights to this expression.
>
> ASCD should address itself to determining and expressing the views of its members on critical contemporary issues. These views should be publicized and used as a basis for ASCD activities that address these issues.[27]

On March 7, 1983, the ASCD Board of Directors adopted the following resolution on a nuclear freeze:

> Aware of the potential devastation and threat to human survival as nuclear weapons multiply in number, range, and power, the citizens of eight of nine states that have recently held referendums have supported nuclear freeze proposals. As educators aware of our responsibility to future generations, ASCD members wish to add moral support to efforts to end an ever-accelerating nuclear arms race.
>
> Therefore, ASCD urges our national government to enter into negotiations to arrive now at an international nuclear freeze accompanied by cooperative international monitoring. ASCD urges full and open discussion in our schools of the nuclear freeze issue and other possible approaches to world peace.[28]

Following the adoption of the resolution on critical contemporary issues, a continuing feature, "Contemporary Issues," was incorporated into the organization's journal, *Educational Leadership*. In addition, a survey on social issues in the curriculum was designed to assess how ASCD members perceived the significance of a variety of social issues and to determine the extent those issues were and should be included in the school curriculum. Survey results were published in the October 1982 issue of *Educational Leadership* as part of the first "Contemporary Issues" feature.[29] The 286 survey responses came from 38 states across the country; several came from Canada and one from West Germany. For the most part, survey respondents were white ASCD members between 30 and 50 years old, and employed in public schools.

As a group, survey respondents (1) considered social issues important, (2) were not satisfied with schools' choices of social issues to study, (3) thought educators should try to formulate positions on social issues and had a social issue they wanted educators to take a position on, (4) felt social issues were not included in the school's curriculum to a great extent, and (5) thought social issues should be included in the social studies curriculum but were somewhat less likely to think they should be a part of the curriculum for other subjects.

The survey data seemed to indicate that respondents perceived social issues as a significant and ill-defined subject territory best explored within the social studies curriculum. Survey results raised interesting questions as to how knowledgeable ASCD members are about specific social issues and the nature and strength of their belief that social issues are primarily a content area within the social studies.

The same survey was administered to National Council for the Social Studies (NCSS) members and to a group of German educators. These survey results seemed to reveal a good deal of dissatisfaction with the ability of professional educators to influence the content of school curriculum at least as it related to social issues. While these results must be treated with caution because they are not derived from statistical samples, they do seem to suggest that further and more controlled follow-up studies are warranted.[30,31] In addition, the data can be used to help formulate questions about the role of social issues in the curriculum and to begin discussions about the proper role of professional organizations in relation to social issues.

It may be that with regard to social issues (which are often controversial), professional educators need to re-think the way in which they conceive of curriculum development. As I have previously noted:

> An examination of school practices provides many possibilities for curriculum development, if teachers learn to use those possibilities. To do so, however, we must move away from reliance on packaged curriculum materials developed by outsiders.... Educational corporations, large and small, peddle their wares regionally and nationally—mainly new stuff in old packages. Any variance in school curriculum is frequently limited to a narrow range of technical modifications within a standard format. We are asked to believe that such modifications are significant in much the same way Burger King would like to believe "that having it our way" somehow makes their product significantly different than that offered by McDonald's who "do it all" for us....

Educators are open to the same criticism that Victor Papanek levels at industrial designers in *Design for the Real World*. He attacks industrial designers for not designing products that people need, products that are straight forward, useful and uncomplicated. In his preface, Papanek proposes that one thing industrial designers could do for humankind would be to stop working entirely. However, he goes on to say: "It seems to me that we can go beyond working at all and work positively. Design can and must become a way in which young people can participate in changing society."[32]

The way for educators to work effectively in curriculum development, particularly when it involves social issues, is to develop close professional relationships with the community they are serving. Too often professional relationships with the public have been characterized by conflict and turmoil. Nevertheless, the difficulties facing educators with regard to social issues in the curriculum must not be understated.

It is a comparatively simple matter for people to identify specific examples of curriculum materials they do not want in their schools, or for researchers such as Harty[33] to warn of the danger posed by free curriculum materials which advocate a particular and biased point of view or for scholars to advocate closer school-community relationships. It is more difficult to untangle relationships that shape and direct what will be taught in schools and define what constitutes a legitimate education. In other words, while it is probably important for professional educators to understand and state their position on the inclusion of controversial topics in school curriculums, it is no doubt equally important for educational scholars to uncover the various mechanisms that result in particular curriculums finding their way into the classroom.

Although educators experience controversy, it is often visited on them for reasons they don't understand, and they feel powerless and frustrated in the face of it. The conflict and turmoil that often surrounds schools is not a historic accident. There are several factors which have affected the historical development, the nature, and the control of American public education. These factors seem to conspire to foster conflict between professional educators and large segments of the public.

It may be helpful to examine the curious fact that although the U.S. does not formally have a national school system, the organization and curriculums of individual American schools are very much alike. The mechanisms which have produced this sameness also may well help to structure in the controversies that seem to rage continuously around public education.

U.S. public schools are not so similar in format and curriculum because they are part of a national school system in which programs are determined and administered by the federal government. Rather, school programs and curriculums are shaped into similar patterns by the explicit influence on and control of public schools and the curriculums by state regulations, by networks of professional affiliation, by the nature of textbook publishing, by federal regulations (concerning such things as racial discrimination, gender equity, and the rights of disabled persons), by accrediting institutions, and by the widespread use of standardized tests. In addition, however, there is another factor of great importance affecting contemporary American social policy in general and educational policy in particular. That factor is the role of large, private, tax-free foundations, which first became a major force in public life toward the end of the 19th century. The foundation form of organization was and is an extremely popular way for large corporations to channel money into projects to achieve social purposes that they deem worthwhile. American public education policy, for example, has been strongly influenced by the Carnegie, Ford, and Rockefeller foundations. What are the characteristics of a project likely to be undertaken by a foundation? Karier quotes Fred M. Hechinger:

> The ideal foundation-sponsored enterprise is one that blazes a new trail, thrives for a while on sponsored dollars, gathers momentum, and is quickly taken over as a permanent program by the local school board, the state education authority, or a university's own budget.[34]

Private Foundations and Education Policy

Karier has argued that foundations in fact represent a fourth branch of government in the U.S. and one that represents the interest of corporate wealth. He points to what is known as "the testing movement" as an example of the power and influence of foundations in American life. The distillation of the concept of equality of opportunity into the belief that a person's standing in society is determined by his or her merit and that school performance is the principal indicator of merit was largely accomplished when it became accepted that intelligence can be measured by standardized tests. The psychologists who developed standardized tests in the U.S., according to Karier, received considerable funding from foundations. Their work has been critical in shaping educational policy. Schools would, so the logic went, be better able to respond to the particular needs and abilities of each student, and to direct each student to the proper work career (assign them to the social position they merited) if they were able to scientifically measure individual ability.

Writing in 1923, Louis M. Terman, one of the leading American developers of standardized tests, reported on his research as follows:

Preliminary investigations indicate that an I.Q. below 70 rarely permits anything better than unskilled labor; that the range 70-80 is pre-eminently that of semi-skilled labor; from 80-100 that of the skilled or ordinary clerical labor; from 100-110 or 115 that of the semi-professional pursuits; and that above all these are the grades of intelligence which permit one to enter the professions or the large fields of business. Intelligence tests can tell us whether a child's native brightness corresponds more nearly to the median of 1) the professional classes, 2) those in the semi-professional pursuits, 3) ordinary skilled workers, 4) semi-skilled workers, or 5) unskilled laborers. This information will be of great value in planning the education of a particular child and also in planning the differentiated curriculum here recommended.[35]

Unfortunately, as Karier points out, the actual content of the intelligence tests upon which Thorndike and other psychometricians of the period based their conclusions reflected a particular world view. This world view was not so very different from that found in, for example, Noah Webster's *American Spelling Book* of the early 19th century. Obviously if standardized intelligence tests had class and cultural bias they would, by definition, discriminate against members of lower classes and minority groups. If school systems then developed programs of academic tracking in which students were placed based on the results of standardized intelligence tests, then the logical consequence would be the creation of the self-fulfilling prophecy. Historically, that is what seems to have happened. Children of lower class parents were told that they had fewer opportunities for success in American society, not because they were members of a class of people that was discriminated against, but because they were, in fact, less capable and did not merit better.

It should be remembered that the emergence of foundations, and the development of the standardized testing movement (which in the U.S. is dated to the mass testing of soldiers who entered the armed forces during World War I) occurred at a time when the problems of industrialization, immigration, and urbanization created enormous political pressure on social policy makers to rationalize social, economic, and political problems. By affirming their particular vision of the orderly development of U.S. society, the policy makers would protect that vision from the perceived dangers imposed by radical and foreign influences.

Although a good many psychologists are now willing to concede that a culture-free test is impossible, others still argue that intelligence tests have value because they predict school success. Thus, while intelligence tests have fallen into a certain disrepute, the idea of standardized testing certainly has not. For example,

While World War I provided a strong stimulus for the testing movement, foundations like the Carnegie Corporation and the Carnegie Foundation for the Advancement of Teaching, Commonwealth Fund, The Graduate Records Office of the Carnegie Foundation, and others, provided the funds that sustained and propelled the movement. World War II demonstrated the usefulness of system analysis and the need, in the name of efficiency, for systematic overall manpower planning. The idea of a centralized testing service.[36]

The centralized testing service described is the Educational Testing Service (ETS) which began in 1947 with a grant from the Carnegie Corporation. Tests developed by ETS, now a private non-profit corporation, are used today to determine the eligibility of millions of Americans to study at colleges and universities and to enter various professions. The fact that ETS is a private organization and that it wields enormous influence reveals in part how social development is influenced by a corporate-professional elite which is not subject to direct political control.

The National Assessment of Educational Progress (NAEP) is a more recent example of how the federal government, private foundations, and the professional community combine forces to shape educational policy.

According to Henderson, during the early 1960s Frances Keppel, then U.S. Commissioner of Education, proposed the idea of a nationwide assessment of what children were learning and the degree of progress of schools in educating American children. In 1964 under the auspices of Carnegie Corporation a group of influential Americans met and founded ECAPE, the Exploratory Committee on Assessing the Progress of Education. The work of this committee was financed for four years entirely by private foundations (although the federal government did provide a grant to the University of Wisconsin to conduct conferences of educators and citizens to respond to and review the work of ECAPE). The work of ECAPE was for several years hindered because the American Association of School Administrators felt that the membership of the group did not represent professional interests. Partially in response to this criticism ECAPE was reconstituted as the Committee on Assessment of Progress in Education (CAPE) with a membership of 25 divided into three constituent groups: members elected by major educational organizations, representatives of public officials, and representatives of the general public. The same year it was founded CAPE was dissolved and the project taken over by the Education Commission of the States which retitled the project "National Assessment of Educational Progress" (NAEP).[37]

The National Assessment is, then, a project jointly conceived by the federal government, private foundations, and the professional educational community, designed to implement a systematic assessment of "the skills, the knowledge, and attitudes of youth and to report the results to all people involved directly or indirectly in the on-going process of improving education."[38]

Whatever the advantages or disadvantages of standardized testing or programs such as NAEP, one thing seems reasonably clear: the fragmentation of political power among local, state, and national levels, the influence of private foundations, and the power of professional educators have created an educational system that is at once similar from school to school in form and content, unequal in the opportunities it provides for children, and relatively isolated from direct, meaningful control by average citizens. Clearly, this is a potentially explosive situation. Consider:

> The most famous school controversy of the early 70's took place in Kanawha County, West Virginia, in September 1974 . . . protestors appeared at the school demanding their closure because of the alleged dirty anti-God, anti-American textbooks. The local coal miners struck in sympathy with the protest. The miners' strike and spreading school boycott resulted in a two million loss, the shooting of two men, firings on school buses, and the bombing of elementary schools. It required state troopers and the FBI to restore order to the school system.[39]

While the Kanawha County incident illustrates how parents and community members are largely cast in the role of reactors to curricular decisions made by others, it also illustrates how narrowly channeled the influence of citizens and parents in an individual school district has become. Local citizens may win a fight or two over the use of this or that textbook, yet meaningful local opposition to the nationwide use of standardized tests, for example, is virtually impossible. Such opposition would require that parents risk hindering their children's education and take on a powerful, well-organized professional, corporate, and political opposition. Furthermore, it would require that parents view the testing of their children both as controversial *and* as a political problem.

One must dismiss as a myth the conventional wisdom that because most of the money for schools is derived from local property taxes, schools are controlled at the local level. According to Sherman, who reviewed studies of school financing, ". . . higher funding levels may not necessarily be associated with more centralized decision-making and . . . a loss of local autonomy does not inevitably result from an increase in state funding."[40] At present, despite the ideal of local control, the U.S. public education system in some ways represents the worst of all possible worlds for poor and working-class Americans. As long as school financing relies on tax revenues tied to local property values, poor and working-class citizens will tend to pay relatively more for their schools and receive relatively less in return. As long as poor and working-class citizens live in different communities than professional, upper-middle and wealthy citizens, their schools will never raise as much money as schools in the wealthier communities. The complex political, private, and professional mechanisms at work in the U.S. provide access for and are responsive to professional, middle-class, and wealthy citizens while poor and working-class citizens are largely excluded from the policy-making process. This means that the poor and working class often pay dearly for schools which they cannot effectively control, and are poorly served by testing processes that tend to screen their children out of meaningful access to what Americans regard as "the good life."[41]

Despite its history of continuing controversy, the public school system is perhaps the closest thing that Americans have to an established church. Indeed, from colonial days when education was often thought of as learning the scriptures, during the early national period when education sought to create "new republican machines," to the late 19th century when schools were asked to "Americanize" millions of immigrant children, to the 20th century institution expected to provide equality of opportunity for every student and to develop programs to help meet social manpower needs, faith in education has been virtually an American dogma. This dogma was severely tested during the 1960s and 70s when a number of social forces combined to place extraordinary pressure on the U.S. school system.

The Challenges of the 1960s and 70s

The reforms of the late 19th and early 20th century had successfully consolidated control of the public schools in the hands of a corporate and professional elite.[42] The thrust of the educational policy demands of black and other minority people, of women, and of political activists in the 60s and 70s was to provide a meaningful equality of access to public schools for all citizens (and through the schools, access to the goods society had to offer); to reform the public schools so that they were more directly responsive to the citizens they were supposed to serve; and to establish alternate forms of education, both public and private. The debates of the 1960s and 1970s were much more broadly referenced in social criticism and more fundamentally critical of the role of school in society than at perhaps any time since the depression of the 1930s.

Richard deLone's analysis of the concept of equality of opportunity from *Small Futures* is an example of the kind of social-educational critique that emerged during the 1960s and 70s:

Americans have sometimes agreed that beyond one-man, one-vote and equal treatment before the law, things are not "as equal" as they should be. But it is always easier to argue that position than to answer "How equal should they be?" Some people maintain that we should pursue absolute equality for all, or equality of condition, but the only clear standard here is the empty concept of mathematical sameness. The more popular and enduring answer has been that society should provide equality of opportunity, specifically that no individual should be denied opportunity by virtue of race, creed, sex, national origin, or other such arbitrary characteristic. But without reference to the end results (which we know to be about as unequal as they ever were in this century), it is no easy task to decide whether equality of opportunity in the competition for social prizes and economic rewards is being achieved. Finally, it is important to remember that "equal opportunity" tells us nothing about equality of condition. To use a simple example, if society consisted of a rich king and 900,000 impoverished subjects, and the king were chosen by lottery, there would be perfect equal opportunity, but little equality to cheer about.[43]

... The persistent belief of liberal reformers has been that it is possible to have your cake and eat it, too; that the elimination of inequality does not depend on redistribution from rich and powerful to poor and powerless; rather, that the way to change society is to change individuals. Liberals have believed that individual reform and economic growth were made for each other, that the interests of the rich and powerful are similar to those of the poor and powerless. Whether or not they were designed as such, these beliefs have been an effective strategy for appeasement. Each time privilege, wealth, corporate power, and extremely unequal distributions of all these have emerged intact.

The ultimate measure of the "success" of these failures is not that the liberal upper-class reformers were always successful in dominating such institutions as schools (although they usually have been) or that they were always able to mold individuals into compliant and industrious workers who blamed only themselves for economic hardship (although they sometimes have). Rather, it is that the premises of liberal reform have been so deeply ingrained in basic social institutions, in the premises of social science, and in our national mythology that efforts to challenge them have trouble even gaining a foothold.

The American emphasis on individual rights and freedom appears to have had high cost—cultural blindness to the significance of social structure and the dynamics of that structure.[44]

As court decision after court decision struck down segregation in the schools; as federal legislation required equal treatment for black and other minorities and women in school programs; as politically active parents organized campaigns for the decentralization of city school systems; and as such programs as educational vouchers were proposed to force schools to be more responsive and more varied in their curricular offerings and instructional strategies, it was clear that even though many had come to regard schools as being controlled by an oppressive social order instead of an agent for changing the social order, public education was still regarded by many Americans as an important vehicle for their participation in American society.

The alternative school movement, which flourished in the U.S. in the 1960s and early 70s, was an attempt to provide options for parents and children who were dissatisfied with curriculum, and/or methods of instruction, and/or the public schools' lack of a particular political point of view, and/or any number of other reasons. That the struggle for access to and control over the public schools was fought at the same time as the struggle for the right to withdraw from public schools probably reflected a growing confusion over the role of public schools. The schools' role could no longer be taken for granted or regarded as self-understood. The challenges and controversies that engulfed the schools in the 1960s and 70s did not spring up overnight. The pressure on the schools to change had been building in society and in the education profession at least since the end of World War II.

After World War II, curriculum problems were perhaps most apparent in urban schools. City schools seemed increasingly unable to educate their poor students, their black students, and their students from other stigmatized groups. This apparent failure was widely believed to be both an effect and a cause of the general social problems faced by the cities themselves.

Curriculum designers were rather slow to respond to growing evidence of a relationship between socio-economic factors and poor performance of city schools. For example, most of the major curriculum reform efforts in the 20 years following World War II failed, by and large, to consider seriously the nature of urban society.[45]

During the mid-1960s, however, dissatisfaction with the performance of urban schools increased and the emphasis of curriculum study shifted. Scholars moved away from their earlier concentration on individual psychology and theories of knowledge and began to study the effect of socio-economic factors on school performance.[46] The period between the mid-1960s and the early 70s was one of widespread experimentation in curriculum design in urban schools. Two general and competing schools of thought emerged. One held that many children did not succeed academically because they were culturally deficient. The role of curriculum was, therefore, to compensate for the social factors which placed those students at a disadvantage academically.[47] The other school of thought held that performance could not be improved appreciably unless curricular reform was linked to social change.[48] Proponents of each position usually agreed, at least tacitly, on two propositions: (1) urban schools were failing, and (2) success in school was central to success in life.

By 1972, the emphasis had begun to shift away from experimentation to evaluation of existing curriculum designs and criticism of the assumptions on which they were based. It was widely accepted that research findings demonstrated that no single curriculum format had proven itself conclusively superior in increasing the overall effectiveness of urban schools.[49] Further, there was less support for the assumption that success in school necessarily leads to success in life.[50]

Some curriculum scholars began to argue that curriculum designs based only on individual psychology, a theory of knowledge, or an analysis of society were inadequate. These scholars believe that curriculum design should be based on an understanding of (1) the relationship among these variables, and (2) the relationship between school success and success in life.[51]

At the moment, there are no widely accepted theoretical conceptions of how curriculum ought to be organized or of the nature of the relationship between school achievement and life success. As a result, researchers continue to pursue diverse lines of inquiry, employing a variety of methodologies. For example, investigations with potentially important implications for the design of urban school curriculum have been conducted to study (1) the nature of human learning styles,[52] (2) the intellectual and affective effects of desegregation,[53] (3) the relationship between socio-cultural factors and achievement in and out of school,[54] and (4) the effect of in-school social variables on achievement.[55] By far the most influential of these new lines of inquiry has been the work on school improvement popularized in the U.S. by Edmonds.[56]

How did public schools adapt and respond to the challenges of the 1960s and 70s? In a variety of ways. It may be helpful to consider the example of how one large city school system, Milwaukee, Wisconsin, responded to court-ordered desegregation of its schools and to the need to reform its curriculum to make it more responsive to the wishes and expectations of students and their parents.

Since most U.S. cities are residentially segregated, school systems ordered by the courts to desegregate often have had to abandon the neighborhood school concept. Although the concept was frequently violated to maintain segregation, its violation for the purpose of integrating the schools aroused considerable controversy. Some school districts, faced with court-ordered desegregation, attempted to develop voluntary programs based on the provision of a variety of curricular alternatives housed in different schools throughout the city. These plans, when they were completely voluntary, tended not to meet expectations. Milwaukee's response to desegregation combined the busing of students to schools outside of their neighborhood with a number of curricular innovations providing parents with a degree of choice about the type of education their children were to receive. For the first time, Milwaukee parents could elect to send their children to elementary schools organized according to open-education principles, Montessori ideas, or along traditional elementary school lines. One elementary school focused on creative arts, another featured language immersion (in which children were taught all subjects entirely either in German or in French), still another offered "basic education" (which enforced strict discipline and emphasized the so-called basics: reading and mathematics). Attendance was determined by parental choice with the limitation that no school could have higher than a certain percentage of black students or lower than a certain percentage of white students.

At the secondary level curricular reform established high schools as centers for particular interests or subjects. For example, Milwaukee now has high schools which emphasize the medical arts, mass communication, computer science, gifted and talented education, the creative and performing arts, and vocational education. Milwaukee high school students must study a basic curriculum regardless of which high school they attend, but are free to pursue their own special interests in more depth. In this way it was hoped that the schools will meet both a common standard and be responsive to the interests of students. As is the case in the elementary schools, students may attend a particular high school on the basis of interest, while the percentages of black and white students at a given high school must fall within a range consistent with the court's desegregation order. Milwaukee created a system of curricular choices that operates within the boundaries imposed by the court's desegregation order.

School systems like Milwaukee's have often attempted to respond creatively to the pressures and demands of the last 15 years. In these attempts they have been aided by federal funds. The economic crisis of the 1970s and 80s, however, has resulted in the withdrawal of public funds from an array of social service enterprises, including public education. This has meant that many school reforms are being undermined for lack of funds. Educational programs in many communities have been reduced to the minimum regarded as necessary to survive. This has meant more students in every classroom, less help for students with special learning needs, and fewer choices for students. While public funds are being cut, public schools are increasingly criticized for not preparing students to compete in the "world of work." Although this criticism defines structural unemployment as a training problem and overlooks the fact that even highly qualified students are often unable to find jobs, it is a logical criticism given the view schools are the principal social mechanism charged with creating equality of opportunity.

Privatization and the Future of Education

In the environment of economic crisis of the 1970s and 80s, the U.S. began to debate with renewed vigor the relationship of public to private education. As I wrote in the April 1984 issue of *Educational Leadership*,[57] the traditional relationship between private and public schools as an important guarantor of educational opportunity and democratic social ideals has, in the past several decades, come increasingly into question. The benefit of this relationship has been challenged in the last 30 years by, among other things, the explosion in the number of all-white private schools in the South after the Supreme Court struck down legally sanctioned segregated schools; the sharp criticism of the public schools in the 60s and 70s for their failure to satisfactorily educate minority poor and working class children; and the development of proposals such as the educational voucher system designed to make public schools more responsive by threatening them with "competition." Most recently the relationship between public and private schools has been threatened by proposals to provide indirect tax support for private schools through tuition tax credits while also reducing federal tax money for public schools as part of a general withdrawal of funds for social welfare programs.

Social welfare policy at the national level in the early 1980s has clearly been based on the assumption that the individual exercise of free choice in an unequal society is the best way of achieving social justice. It would be a mistake, however, to describe this ideology (given the social history of the U.S.) as conservative in a partisan sense. Political liberals and conservatives have always shared this ideological premise. They have differed only on the extent to which it should be carried through in social policy.

The guiding ideology of social welfare policy in the 1980s can be characterized by the term "privatization," putting as much money as possible in private hands so that every individual can determine for himself or herself how best to spend it. It is argued that this will revitalize unresponsive, inefficient public bureaucracies, and unleash the productive capacity of our capitalist economy. The ideology of privatization and its potential impact on legislation and social programs is perhaps the central issue facing educational policy makers today.

Privatization is an especially important issue for educators because of the historical significance of education in public life. Existing alongside of tax-supported public schools, self-supporting private schools have contributed to the development of social democracy. Private schools, which in some instances predate the Republic, are held to demonstrate, by their existence, that intellectual and religious freedom is a reality. Further, in the case of church schools, the fact that they must be self-supporting has been a concrete representation of the constitutional separation of church and state. Americans have traditionally tended not only to regard education as a common good, they have also regarded the development of both private and public schools as the best way to assure that good in a pluralistic democracy. The historical experience of the United States has contrasted sharply with that of Great Britain where private schools have been characterized by Labour Party leader Neil Kinnock as "the very cement in the wall that divides British society."

Rarely has the need to develop a structural analysis in order to understand such social policy issues as the proper relationship between the public and private provision of social welfare services been so clear. For years U.S. social policy makers have used structurally irrelevant differences between liberal and conservative interpretations of the republican social vision of the 19th and early 20th century to keep conflict within acceptable bounds. It now appears, however, that the economic restructuring of the capitalist world is threatening to break down the old boundaries. For example, in 1982 republican and democratic politicians worked to "reform" the Social Security system. In the process their public pronouncements encouraged Americans to regard the primary problem of the Social Security system as administrative and/or demographic rather than mass unemployment. They further eroded public confidence in, and political support for, the system by supporting legislation to enable those with enough money to set up tax-sheltered Individual Retirement Accounts (IRAs). These accounts amount to a hidden tax on the working poor who must help make up for tax dollars lost due to these accounts and who do not have enough money to benefit from them. In other words, as liberals and conservatives are forced to move closer and closer together in their social policy formulations, the practical result is a continued deepening of the class divisions in American society and the potential for increased danger of social conflict of the sort that social welfare programs and public education are supposed to render unnecessary.

The relationship between the Social Security system and IRAs is structured in roughly the same way as the new relationship that could apply between public and private schools if the government grants tax credits for private school tuition. In the absence of political support for a social policy aimed at the structural reform of American society, such moves to "privatize" social services would be likely to accelerate the withdrawal of public money for such social welfare programs as public education. This would in turn tend to put an increasing amount of money in the pockets of a relatively wealthy minority who could then privately purchase a variety of social services from trash collection to good schools for their children. At the same time, the majority of citizens would face the loss of an increasing number of social welfare benefits or would have to reduce their standard of living to pay for them.

These historical circumstances place educators in a paradoxical situation. Most professional educators probably consider themselves middle class. However, since their middle class status has been brought about to a large extent by public tax support, *individual* educators could profit from the privatization of social services through such schemes as IRAs, yet their professional status and membership in the middle class would be threatened by such a shift in social policy.[58] To pose the problem concretely, educators in the 1980s will be confronted with determining whether they will support a social policy that enables them to open Individual Retirement Accounts or whether they will attempt to formulate a social policy that enables the equal provision of education for all children through the adequate and equalized financing of public schools. Clearly the controversy and struggle that have characterized the development of the public school system are going to continue through the 1980s.

The Continuing Controversy

What could or should the public schools look like in the years to come, and what forces will shape them? Perhaps Kaestle has as clear a vision as anyone:

> I believe that we need the unified, tax-supported, common-school system. I believe that the public school systems of our states and localities need to be more common in some respects, that is, more equal and more integrated. But they also need to be much more diverse in other respects, more open to different teaching and learning styles, different cultural content, different parental preferences, and different community needs. Like most people, I agree with some aspects of cosmopolitan school reform and central control while I disagree with others. My personal inclination is to support cosmopolitan solutions on constitutional issues like separation of church and state, equal rights, and free expression, which requires staunch central protection whatever the views of local majorities. I am more skeptical and selective about supporting the standardization of curriculum, program organization, or learning style, which is often argued on grounds of efficiency, upgrading standards, or the superior abilities of central decision makers. The apportioning of authority among federal, state, and local levels is a delicate matter, one which will continue to be debated in the decades ahead. But that is good. Centralization should not be mindless drift or merely a matter of who is more powerful. We need not be trapped by history, nor by the language of modernization and efficiency. We must be imaginative about the control of schools.
>
> When the American colonies asked England to give their legislatures independent authority on some matters, Parliament replied that there was no such thing as absolute authority within an absolute authority. "Imperium in imperio," they said, was an impossibility. For that lack of imagination they lost the American

colonies. The history of American federalism is one of constantly evolving
relationships between local, state and national governments, conditioned but
not mechanically determined by technological, economic, political, constitutional and cultural changes. . . . The adjustment of the claims and powers of the
different levels of government is an imperfect, a continual, and a bruising
process. It is one of the central dynamics of American educational history and
of American political life.[59]

To Kaestle's vision I would add that the recent struggles over access to
and financing for public schools; the continuing fight over the proper relationship between federal, state, and local governments in forming educational
policy; and the proper role of foundations and quasi-public institutions such
as the Educational Testing Service will, no doubt, continue to be strongly
influenced by economic developments. The economic crises of the last 10
years and the attendant long-term high rates of unemployment challenge the
conventional American view of the school as a merocratic mechanism of social
betterment, in the sense that a good education is what allows one to climb
out of the lower class. Nevertheless, the gatekeeping and certification functions
of schools are likely to ensure the continued intense competition for school
credentials. Throughout all of this education professionals will be challenged
to define their position and their role with regard to a whole array of social
policy issues.

Although such a development is not likely in the near future, it is interesting to contemplate what form public education would take if social policy
confronted directly the problem of providing enough work for every citizen
instead of concentrating on demanding that citizens compete for an inadequate number of jobs. Such a social policy would challenge the assumption
that one must "climb out" of the working class to have a decent and secure
life and its educational corollary: equality of opportunity. The meaning of
public education in a democratic society that is based on egalitarian principles
is a challenge the U.S. has yet to seriously consider . . . and a proposition
guaranteed to produce controversy.

Social issues have been and are likely to remain uncomfortable for
professional educators because they are controversial and because there are
few clear and agreed upon guidelines for what exactly educators should *do*
with them. Nevertheless, social issues, uncomfortable and controversial as
they often are, are important for educators to consider critically because they
reflect important aspects of the social context in which schools are expected
to function and they often represent potential claims for inclusion in the
school curriculum. Given the nature of our republican democracy and the
historic role of schools in moderating social tensions, it is inevitable that every

social issue will continue to be a potential policy and curriculum problem for educators.

Notes

[1]David B. Tyack, *Turning Points in American Educational History* (Waltham, Mass.: Blaisdell Publishing Co., 1967), p. 83.

[2]Carl F. Kaestle, *Pillars of the Republic: Common Schools and American Society 1780-1860* (New York: Hill and Wang, 1983), p. 7.

[3]Ibid.

[4]Richard H. deLone, *Small Future: Inequality and the Limits of Liberal Reform* (New York: Harcourt, Brace, Jovanovich, 1979), p. 36.

[5]Ibid., p. 40.

[6]Ibid., p. 44.

[7]Michael B. Katz, *Class Bureaucracy and Schools: The Illusion of Educational Change in America* (New York: Praeger Publishers, 1971), p. 7.

[8]Ibid., p. 52.

[9]Tyack, p. 354.

[10]Ibid., p. 352.

[11]Daniel Tanner, "The American High School at the Crossroads," *Educational Leadership* 41 (March 1984): 5.

[12]Katz, pp. 27, 28.

[13]Tyack, p. 127.

[14]Ibid., pp. 358-361.

[15]National Education Association, *Report of the Committee of Ten on Secondary School Studies* (New York: Arno Press, 1969).

[16]Commission on the Reorganization of Secondary Education of the National Education Association, "Cardinal Principles of Secondary Education" (Washington, D.C.: Department of the Interior, Bureau of Education Bulletin No. 35, 1918).

[17]National Policies Commission of the National Education Association, *Education for ALL American Youth* (Washington, D.C.: National Education Association, 1944.)

[18]Jerome Bruner, *The Process of Education* (Cambridge: Harvard University Press, 1960).

[19]Educational Policies Commission of the National Education Association, *The Central Purpose of American Education* (Washington, D.C.: National Education Association, 1961).

[20]John Dewey, *Democracy and Education* (New York: The Free Press, 1966).

[21]George S. Counts, *Dare the Schools Build a New Social Order?* (New York: Arno Press, 1969).

[22]Bruner, *The Process of Education*.

[23]H. G. Rickover, *American Education—A National Failure* (New York: Dutton, 1963).

[24]James S. Coleman and others, *Equality of Educational Opportunity* (Washington, D.C.: U.S. Department of Health, Education and Welfare, 1966).

[25]Charles Silberman, *Crisis in the Classroom* (New York: Random House, Inc., 1970).

[26]Consider the following books and reports published in 1983: *Academic Preparation for College: What Students Need to Know and Be Able to Do* (New York: College Entrance Examination Board); *Action for Excellence: A Comprehensive Plan to Improve Our Nation's Schools* (Denver: Education Commission of the States, Task Force on Education for Economic Growth); *A Nation at Risk: The Imperative for Educational Reform* (Washington, D.C.: National Commission on Excellence in Education); John I. Goodlad, *A Place Called School: Prospects for the Future* (New York: McGraw-Hill Book Company); National Science Board Commission on Precollege Education in Mathematics, Educating Americans for the 21st Century (Washington, D.C.: National Science Foundation.

[27]"ASCD Resolution on Critical Contemporary Issues," *Educational Leadership* 40 (April 1983): 38.

[28]"ASCD Resolution on Nuclear Freeze," *Educational Leadership* 40 (May 1983): 42.

[29]Alex Molnar, "A Report to the Membership on the Survey on Social Issues and School Curriculum," *Educational Leadership* 40 (April 1983): 51-54. The "Contemporary Issues" featured in *Educational Leadership* have included such topics as nuclear disarmament, world hunger, environmental pollution—and their significance for educators.

[30]Alex Molnar, "Are the Issues Studied in School the Important Issues Facing Humankind?" *Social Education* 47 (May 1983): 305-307.

[31]Alex Molnar and others, "West German Teachers on Today's Issues," *Social Education* 48 (September/October 1984): 400-404. An extended discussion of these results will be published in West Germany in *Westermans Pädagogische beiträge* under the title "Wie Aktuell ist die Schule."

[32]Alex Molnar, "Progressive School-Community Relationships as a Basis for Changing Educational Practice," in *Community Participation in Education*, ed. Carl Grant (Boston: Allyn and Bacon, 1979): 248-249.

[33]Sheila Harty, *Hucksters in the Classroom* (Washington, D.C.: Center for the Study of Responsive Law, 1979).

[34]Clarence J. Karier, "Testing for Order and Control in the Corporate Liberal State," in *Roots of Crisis: American Education in the Twentieth Century*, eds. C. J. Karier, Paul Violas, and J. Spring (Chicago: Rand McNally, 1973), p. 110.

[35]Ibid., p. 121.

[36]Ibid., p. 134.

[37]George Henderson, *Introduction to American Education* (Norman: University of Oklahoma Press, 1978). For a detailed discussion of the background to the National Assessment and the National Assessment process, see Chapter 8.

[38]Finley and Berdie in "The National Assessment Approach to Exercise Development" as quoted in Henderson, *Introduction to American Education*, p. 166.

[39]Joel Spring, *American Education: An Introduction to Social and Political Aspects* (New York: Longman, 1978), p. 103.

[40]Joel D. Sherman, "Changing Patterns of School Finance," in *Government in the Classroom: Dollars and Power in Education*, ed. M. F. Williams (New York: Praeger Publishers, 1979), p. 72.

[41]For a detailed account of how testing practices vary for children from different social class backgrounds, see Kenneth Wodtke and others, "The Mismeasure of Young

Children: Is There Malpractice in Early School Testing?" Research report prepared for presentation at the 1985 meeting of the American Educational Research Association.

[42]See, for example, the discussion of the composition of state and local boards of education in Joel Spring, *American Education: An Introduction to the Social and Political Aspects*, and Ralph B. Kimbrough and Michael J. Nunnery, *Educational Administration: An Introduction* (New York: Collier, 1976).

[43]deLone, p. 24.

[44]deLone, pp. 76-77.

[45]See, for example, Bruner, *The Process of Education*; John I. Goodlad and Maurice N. Richter, Jr., *The Development of a Conceptual System for Dealing with Problems of Curriculum and Instruction* (Los Angeles: University of California, 1966); Ralph W. Tyler, *Basic Principles of Curriculum and Instruction* (Chicago: University of Chicago Press, 1949).

[46]James S. Coleman and others, *Equality of Educational Opportunity*.

[47]Carl C. Mack, Jr., "Old Assumptions and New Packages: Racism, Education Models, and Black Children," *Young Children* 33 (September 1978): 45-51.

[48]See, for example, Ray C. Rist, "Student Social Class and Teacher Expectations: The Self-Fulfilling Prophecy in Ghetto Education," *Harvard Educational Review* 40 (August 1970): 411-451; Stephen S. Baratz and Joan C. Baratz, "Early Childhood Intervention: The Social Base of Institutional Racism," *Harvard Educational Review* 40 (Winter 1970): 19-50.

[49]Decker F. Walker and Jon Schaffarzik, "Comparing Curricula," *Journal of Educational Research* 44 (Winter 1974): 83-111.

[50]Christopher Jencks and others, *Inequality* (New York: Basic Books, 1972).

[51]See, for example, Dwayne Huebner, "The Tasks of the Curriculum Theorist" in *Curriculum Theorizing*, ed. W. Pinar (Berkeley: McCutchan, 1975); James B. Macdonald, "Value Bases and Issues for Curriculum" in *Curriculum Theory*, eds. A. Molnar and J. Zahorik (Washington, D.C.: Association for Supervision and Curriculum Development, 1977).

[52]Lee Cronbach and Richard Snow, *Aptitudes in Instructional Methods: A Handbook for Research on Interactions* (New York: Irvington Publishers, 1977).

[53]Nancy H. St. John, *School Desegregation: Outcomes for Children* (New York: John Wiley and Sons, 1975).

[54]See, for example, Michael W. Apple and Nancy King, "What Do Schools Teach?" in *Humanism and Schooling*, eds. J. B. Macdonald and W. Gephard (Berkeley: McCutchan, 1978); Basil B. Bernstein, *Class Pedagogies, Visible and Invisible* (Paris: Organization for Economic Cooperation and Development, 1975); Ulf Lundgren and Sten Pettersson, eds., *Code, Context, and Curriculum Processes* (Stockholm: Stockholm Institute of Education, 1979); John Ogbu, *Minority Education and Caste: The American System in Cross Cultural Perspective* (New York: Academic Press, 1978).

[55]Wilbur B. Brookover, John H. Schweitzer, and others, "Elementary School Social Climate and School Achievement," *American Educational Research Journal* 15 (Spring j1978): 301-318.

[56]Ronald R. Edmonds, "Programs of School Improvement: An Overview," *Educational Leadership* 40 (December 1982): 4-11.

[57]Alex Molnar, "High Quality Public Education or Individual Retirement Accounts: Which Side Are You On?" *Educational Leadership* 41 (April 1984): 55-57.

[58]For a thorough discussion of the conflicting positions of teachers in a capitalist social system, see Keven Harris, *Teachers and Classes* (London: Routledge and Kegan Paul, 1982).

[59]Kaestle, pp. 224-225.

Chapter 2.
Three Currents of American Curriculum Thought

HERBERT M. KLIEBARD

Thinking about the curriculum is as old as thinking about education. It is hard to imagine any inquiry into the nature of education without deliberate attention to the question of what should be taught. From the point of view of a serious educator, whatever the historical period or the particular setting, the question of what to teach involves a selection from a vast array of knowledge and belief within a culture. Since it is impossible to teach everything, that selection from the culture reflects in part some sense of what is most worthwhile in that culture seen in relation to the kind of institution the school is and what it can reasonably accomplish. In *The Republic*, for example, Plato thought that the young men of Athens ought to study geometry because, in his view, "a training in geometry makes all the difference in preparing the mind for any kind of study."[1] Plato was thus arguing the case for geometry over other possible subjects of study and supporting his particular choice with what he assumed to be a sound reason for that choice. In this same manner, many curriculum decisions are made today but with other kinds of evidence being cited for those choices.

Aristotle recognized the complexity of deciding what to teach:

> At present, opinion is divided about the subjects of education. All do not take the same view about what should be learned by the young, either with a view

Herbert M. Kliebard is Professor, Department of Educational Policy Studies, University of Wisconsin-Madison.

to plain goodness or with a view to the best life possible; nor is opinion clear whether education should be directed mainly to the understanding, or mainly to moral character. If we look at actual practice, the result is sadly confusing; it throws no light on the problem whether the proper studies to be followed are those which are useful in life, or those which make for goodness, or those which advance the bounds of knowledge. Each sort of study receives some votes in its favour.[2]

Beyond its quaint phrasing Aristotle's statement has an unusually modern ring, capturing something of the timelessness of the questions that have pervaded the study of curriculum since ancient times. In particular, he drew attention to the fact that curriculum decisions inevitably involve questions of value. What sometimes appears to be a straightforward choice from the various subjects of study brings us into the realm of differing value systems. Even in settled periods in history, questions about what knowledge should be passed on to the young involve conflicting ideals and values, but in periods of rapid social change, those questions become particularly urgent and puzzling.

The era we now know as the Renaissance, for example, not only was a period of profound social change and a rebirth of learning but also one in which great thinkers were writing pedagogical tracts that attempted to define what the youth of Europe should be studying. Desiderius Erasmus, Vittorino da Feltre, Joannes Ludovicus Vives, and François Rabelais all wrote major treatises on curriculum. Rabelais's *Gargantua* and *Pantagruel* conceived of the curriculum as an enormous feast filled not only with the delicacies of Greek, Latin, Chaldean, Hebrew, and Arabic but also with musical accomplishment, physical prowess, knowledge of metals and precious gems, and even the casting of artillery. His work represents a break with a traditionally narrow and constricted curriculum. The work of Erasmus in *De Ratione Studii* and of Vives in *De Tradendis Disciplinis*, while also departing from the traditional scholastic curriculum, point in a somewhat different direction—mainly toward literary and linguistic elegance. Although in periods of change there may be agreement on the need for a reconstruction of the curriculum, it would be rare indeed for there to be any sort of unanimity on the direction the curriculum should take. What tends to emerge from the desire to change the curriculum in a changing society is a compromise among different and even competing programs for reform.

The 20th-century American curriculum emerged most directly from a period of unrest in the 1890s when there appeared to be a profound realization on the part of American leaders and the general public that a major transformation had been wrought in American society. Although the social changes themselves had been in progress for several decades, during the 1890s the perception of change became particularly acute. Urbanization, mass immigration, and immense industrial growth were themselves highly significant; but, in addition, a vast increase in railroad travel and in newspaper and magazine circulation meant that the awareness of social change was being brought home to ever larger segments of the American population. The major depression of 1893 added an ominous note to this perception of change, and Americans generally were beginning to worry about what kind of world the 20th century would bring. Labor unrest, vice in the cities, corruption in government, and what was seen as undesirable immigration from southern and eastern Europe led to fears that a fragile society would soon come apart.

It was in this context that Americans looked more and more to schools as a vehicle for addressing these problems. While the traditional humanist curriculum engendered some dissatisfaction during the 19th century, it nonetheless remained fairly stable, bolstered in large measure by the theory of mental discipline. When certain subjects, such as the classical languages, were criticized for being impractical or even useless, as was the case with the controversy over the Yale College curriculum in 1828,[3] there was always recourse to a justification similar to that espoused by Plato: certain subjects had the power to develop the mind more than others, and development of the various faculties of the mind, such as memory, reasoning, and imagination, was the chief function of schooling. Thus, a combination of the humanistic ideal and a belief that powers of the mind needed to be trained through vigorous exercise helped support existing curricular practices.

Apart from the social changes that were being so keenly felt in the 1890s, one immediate factor that created the climate for reconsideration of the existing curriculum was the sheer increase in the number of children entering school, particularly adolescents. In 1890 less than 7 percent of adolescents from 14 to 17 attended school; within a scant four decades more than half of adolescents that age were in secondary schools. It was becoming problematic as to whether the curriculum that had served so successfully in the 19th century would be suitable for the new population of students then marching through the schoolhouse doors. Among those wary of that possibility were such prominent psychologists as E. L. Thorndike, whose experiments indicated that many assumptions of faculty psychology were not borne out by experimental testing.[4]

Challenges to the old order in curriculum matters were coming from a variety of sources. The issue achieved national visibility in 1892, when the National Education Association appointed a committee of prominent educators to study the question of uniformity in high school programs of study. The committee was headed by the highly respected president of Harvard University, Charles W. Eliot, a mental disciplinarian but one who saw that theory as capable of adjusting to the demands of modern education. The report that the Committee of Ten issued in 1893 represented a modest compromise between established tradition in curriculum matters and calls for a dramatic change. The committee set up four model "programmes," which by contemporary standards are thoroughly academic, but in their time represented something of a movement away from the standard curriculum of the day. The committee, for example, accepted modern foreign languages as the virtual equivalent of Latin and Greek, thus departing from the commonly held view that the classical languages were disciplinary while French and German were simply practical.

Although the committee is often accused of imposing college domination of the curriculum in secondary schools, the members actually saw themselves as developing a curriculum for "life" and only incidentally for admission to college. Such a curriculum for life in their view developed the intellectual capacities of all students regardless of probable destination. Eliot was especially wary of early curriculum "bifurcation" into college-going and non-college-going populations, which he regarded as a form of prognostication that could easily become a self-fulfilling prophecy.

Although the Committee of Ten report received much approbation in its day, its most fundamental recommendations essentially were rejected by 20th-century curriculum makers. The vast majority of educational leaders favored a change in curriculum that would parallel what they saw as the massive change that had been wrought in American society. That drive for a thorough reformulation of the curriculum in the 20th century is what many latter-day interpreters see as the progressive education movement. But when that desire for change is seen in the light of differing and even competing ideals and value systems held by educational reformers of the period, competing values of the sort that Aristotle noted, then it becomes well-nigh impossible to define a single coherent educational-reform movement. What we find instead is that when the recognition of a need for change is filtered through the lenses of people with differing political and social orientations, proposals for reform of quite different character and intent emerge.

The Social Efficiency Ideal

In general, three major challenges to the humanistic and plainly academic curriculum reaffirmed by the Committee of Ten began to emerge in the 1890s and survived through at least most of the 20th century. The most powerful of these movements was one that sought to redefine the curriculum in line with the tenets of social efficiency. Had the program of the social efficiency educators been fully implemented, the effect on the curriculum would have been revolutionary. In social terms, however, the basic thrust of the movement was conservative. For proponents of social efficiency, a major part of their opposition to the standard academic curriculum of the day derived from what they perceived as its sheer uselessness. It was difficult, from their point of view, to discern in the daily lives of people any relevance to the study of foreign languages, higher mathematics, physics, or masterworks of literature that dominated the curriculum. Accordingly, they sought to build a taut connection between what was studied in school and the everyday lives of people. To major leaders of the movement such as Franklin Bobbitt, W. W. Charters, and David Snedden, this meant a careful analysis of the actual activities that people performed in the course of their work, play, home life, and as citizens that would provide the basis for what to teach. Of the three major reform movements that had some impact on the American curriculum of the 20th century, social efficiency was probably the most anti-academic.

One major manifestation of the social efficiency ideal was the *Cardinal Principles Report* of 1918.[5] Prepared by a National Education Association committee, it differed markedly from the Committee of Ten's report only a quarter century earlier. Completely absent was the mental disciplinarian justification for school subjects, now replaced by a frank appeal to utility and good citizenship. The value of school studies would not be measured by their ability to strengthen the mental faculties but by the extent to which they would contribute to seven aims of secondary education: health, command of fundamental processes, worthy home membership, vocation, citizenship, worthy use of leisure, and ethical character. Each of the subjects, it was urged, should be able to demonstrate its contribution to the achievement of these seven aims or face the danger of elimination. In practice, a subject like literature could make a claim to worthy use of leisure and history to informed citizenship, but clearly the subjects in the most advantageous position were the ones that appeared to have the most direct relationship to the duties of life.

The *Cardinal Principles Report* achieved wide acclaim not only when it was first issued but also for many decades thereafter. Part of its popularity may be attributed to the fact that Clarence Kingsley, in formulating the recommendations, avoided the extremes that many of the leaders of the social-efficiency movement were recommending. Snedden, Kingsley's close colleague, favored a dual system of secondary education involving a separate system of vocational education along the German model. Early division along academic and vocational lines was much more efficient in determining what should be taught. But Kingsley strongly favored the comprehensive high school with differentiated curriculums, not separate institutions attuned to the different educational requirements of high school students. Kingsley also stopped short of eliminating academic subjects altogether for the majority of high school students, a course of action that was also widely recommended. Instead, he advocated that subjects be adapted so as to be more directly functional.

The social efficiency movement as a form of curriculum thinking had two great appeals. The first was to efficiency itself. During the first quarter of the 20th century, efficiency became a watchword in industry through the work of Frederick Winslow Taylor and his disciples, and thus became, to some, almost synonymous with science. Scientific curriculum-makers, as they liked to call themselves, like Bobbitt and Charters, became enormously influential in their efforts to trim the curriculum of its dead wood. Their technique of curriculum making, the analysis of activity, was essentially borrowed from Taylorism and represented for them a scientific way to determine what should be taught just as scientific management replaced older, less efficient approaches to production in industry. After careful study of what people did in life, a curriculum scientifically attuned to their needs could be constructed in the same way that the most efficient route to production could be discovered by careful observation of the workers' motions.

The second appeal to social efficiency was more subtle. It was the appeal to social stability in a society where many of the earlier mechanisms of social control were losing their potency. The school was seen not so much as an institution where mental development would be fostered as the Committee of Ten had advocated, but as a place where the individual would be prepared to assume a specific social role. By conceiving of the curriculum as a vehicle for training individuals to perform effectively in their assigned societal roles, social efficiency as a curriculum doctrine held out the promise of an orderly and well-run society. In order to accomplish this, early determination of future role was necessary, a course that Eliot had vigorously opposed in 1893, but which, by the second decade of the 20th century, mass mental testing had made a much more plausible option.

A Curriculum Attuned to Human Development

A second movement for reform of curriculum thinking also represented itself as having the backing of science, but it was a far different science from that borrowed from scientific management. Basically, this developmentalist movement sought the key to the curriculum riddle by deriving the course of study from the natural order of development in the child. Once we knew the secrets of child and adolescent development, we could develop a curriculum based on the natural inclinations and ways of thinking that are part of the child's make-up. The idea that individuals passed through stages of development with distinctive characteristics is, of course, centuries old. Its application to education and particularly to the question of what to teach was elaborately treated in Rousseau's *Emile* in the late 18th century, and reemerged in a particularly powerful form in American curriculum thinking in the late 19th century.

One source of the new thinking about the curriculum was the American disciples of Johann Friedrich Herbart such as Charles De Garmo and Frank McMurry who had studied at the great centers of pedagogy in Germany and returned to the United States with a zealous desire to reform American education. They rejected the dominant psychology of the day, faculty psychology, in favor of an approach that attempted to capitalize on children's interests and eliminated much of the monotonous drill and teacher imposition that they felt dominated American schools. Through their concept of apperception, they sought to tie what was learned to the existing cognitive structure, and so it became extremely important to know what was already in the child's mind before proceeding with anything new. In their search for a curriculum tied to the child's natural predilections, they frequently employed the concept of culture epochs, the notion that there was almost an exact parallel between the stages of human history and the maturational stages of the individual. Thus very young children would be interested in myths and legends because our early ancestors with whom they were somehow affiliated used them to explain their world. Similarly, children were believed to pass through distinct periods such as a savage stage and an agricultural stage, each with important implications for what curriculum materials would be most appropriate at given ages.

In the 1870s, the cause of child-study gained impetus through the criticism of American education advanced by Charles Francis Adams,[6] especially by his efforts to draw attention to the child's mental habits as a way of bringing the light of science to a benighted pedagogy. Adams' high praise for the work of Colonel Francis Parker in the Quincy, Massachusetts, school system not only brought Parker national prominence, but seemed to indicate that drudgery and repression were not necessary concomitants of schooling. Parker had not simply introduced a much greater measure of freedom for the child than was typical of the regimented schools of that time. He had essentially discarded the old course of study in favor of one that was congenial to the child's penchant for play and activity. He introduced what he called the "word method" of teaching reading, which replaced drill in phonics with what Parker considered the natural way by which children learned language. Word problems in arithmetic were favored over the mere manipulation of numbers, and rules and generalizations were reserved for the later periods of schooling. Formal grammar in the early grades was also discontinued, and natural language activities such as letter writing were introduced. The Quincy schools were held up by Adams as a model of schooling, not only because the natural predilections of the child could be used to enrich the spirit of the school, but because effective learning was taking place.

Of the numerous proponents of child study in the late 19th century, however, none was more prominent than G. Stanley Hall. Upon his return from study in Germany in 1880, he quickly became the most prestigious psychologist in the country. Like the social efficiency educators, Hall and his fellow developmentalists rejected the recommendations of the Committee of Ten report, especially its emphasis on the training of the intellect as the primary function of schooling. Hall felt that reasoning power was not yet in the child's repertoire and that early concentration on intellectual matters could be injurious to the child's health. Unlike the social efficiency reformers, he took the position that the school must first and foremost stay out of the child's way, and that one way of preventing harm to the child was to prolong the period of childhood rather than to point too quickly to adult life. Hall's curriculum would be dominated by play at least until the eighth year, and drill and memorization would be preferable to the attempt to teach reasoning since, according to his studies, the child was not capable of reason until a much later age.

Hall's vision of a curriculum carefully attuned to the natural development of children and adolescents, despite its persistent call to scientific validity, was infused with rampant sentimentality and a high romanticism. His mystical beliefs in race recapitulation, derived from the Herbartian concept of culture epochs, were often wildly far-fetched, and by the beginning of the 20th century his influence began to wane. The appearance, however, of "The Project Method" by William Heard Kilpatrick in 1918 gave fresh impetus to the idea that the child could, after all, become the center for curriculum making.[7] Although the idea of developing a curriculum around projects rather than subjects had been gathering momentum for about a dozen years before he published his article, Kilpatrick's ideas served to broaden its scope beyond its origins in vocational agriculture to the curriculum as a whole. Projects were designed to capitalize on children's interests and to make them active learners. Content in the curriculum played a distinctly secondary role usually acquired in the context of the child's own "purposing." Contrary to the main precepts of social efficiency, projects emphasized the child's own present orientation rather than future adult roles. Kilpatrick's enormous popularity as a professor at

Teachers College, Columbia University, and his prolific writing put him, a philosopher rather than a psychologist, in the forefront of the effort to reform the curriculum in line with the natural unfolding of the child's mind and personality. As the movement progressed, what was once known simply as the project method was elaborated into the activity curriculum or the experience curriculum. Those forms of curriculum organization, while not replacing the standard subject organization, had some impact within the context of subject areas such as English and social studies.

The Road to Social Meliorism

The third major reform movement in curriculum also had its origins around the turn of the century, although it remained a largely subterranean movement except for one brief period of prominence in the 1930s. In 1896, John Dewey's colleague at the University of Chicago, the great American sociologist Albion Small, delivered a paper before the annual meeting of the National Education Association. Three years after the report of the Committee of Ten was issued, Small began his address by apologizing for reopening "a closed incident of ancient history" in using that committee's recommendations as a vehicle for proposing a different conception of a proper course of study.[8]

Small was particularly disturbed by the report of the Conference on History, Civil Government, and Political Economy, a subcommittee that had included among its members James Harvey Robinson and Woodrow Wilson. Small interpreted its report as assuming that the purpose of education was, first of all, "completion of the individual," and secondly, "adaption of the individual to such cooperation with the society in which his lot is cast that he works at his best with the society in perfecting his own type. . . ."[9] The report, Small felt, presented a "classified catalogue of subjects good for study" without any real social philosophy. If the report offered any conception of education as a whole, it was dominated by "a naively mediaeval psychology . . . which would be humorous if it were not tragical."[10] Such a dependence on faculty psychology led the committee to believe, according to Small, that history can train the faculty called judgment, that mathematics hones the faculty called reasoning, and so on as if powers of the mind existed as isolated entities and intelligence itself were somehow separated from the rest of existence. "Education," he claimed, "connotes the evolution of the whole personality, not merely of intelligence."[11]

Small argued that students must be taught to see the whole if they are to make any sense or derive any meaning from the abstractions that these subjects presumably represent. "Knowledge so far as it is gained at all," Small emphasized, must be seen in relationships, "not as self-sufficient knowledges."[12] Not simply the study of sociology, but all branches of knowledge should begin at the heart of concentric circles of social activity starting with the household and gradually extending outward until the social *desideratum* is finally reached, whereby "the developing member of the society shall become analytically and synthetically intelligent about the society to which he belongs."[13] He concluded his address with a strong endorsement of education as a vehicle of social amelioration. Contrary to the position endorsed by the child-study advocates, he insisted that educators "shall not rate themselves leaders of children, but as makers of society. Sociology knows no means for the amelioration or reform of society more radical than those of which the teachers hold the leverage."[14] In general, Small's ideas reflected not simply the growing impatience with the traditional course of study, but more particularly his ideas foreshadowed a growing tendency to see education not simply in terms of individual development of intellectual powers or even encouraging the child's natural tendencies to unfold, but in terms of social progress. Unlike the social efficiency educators who viewed the social role of the school as a tool of societal stability, Small and those who followed his lead saw the schools as a lever for social rejuvenation.

Small's vision of the schools as an instrument of social reform can be detected in the early work of John Dewey and George S. Counts during the first two decades of the 20th century, but it did not become a potent force on the national educational scene until the Great Depression of the 1930s once more raised doubts about the ability of the economic structure to survive. Until that time, curriculum reform was dominated by the opposing ideals represented by social efficiency and child growth and development tempered by the existing structure of schools, which tended to favor the traditional curriculum organization recommended by the Committee of Ten. In that sense the standard curriculum remained surprisingly resilient to the zealous efforts of the reformers. Probably the most significant curriculum change of the early 20th century was the introduction on a massive scale of vocational education advocated by social efficiency educators, particularly specific occupational training. In line with the social meliorist position enunciated by Small, Jane Addams and Dewey had argued unsuccessfully that industrial education should educate future workers about the nature of the industrial process and of an industrial society.

When the Progressive Education Association was organized in 1919, its platform reflected the romantic ideal of childhood imbedded in the developmentalist position of Hall and later Kilpatrick. It was not until the 1930s that prominent professors of education, drawn largely from faculty of Teachers

College, Columbia University, succeeded in diverting the central purpose of the PEA away from its child-centered ideal to an emphasis on social concerns. Epitomized by Count's clarion call, "Dare the Schools Build a New Social Order?"[15] the new leaders of the PEA sought a curriculum that would address directly the social and economic ills that beset American life. Despite the prominence of the leaders of the social reconstructionist movement and the fact that the social conditions of the time were congenial to a radical reformulation of the curriculum, there were few notable successes. Most school administrators and teachers simply did not share the ideas being promulgated by a small group of eastern intellectuals. Clearly the most successful of the efforts of the social meliorists was the wide adoption of a series of 14 social studies textbooks written by Harold Rugg. In a deliberate attempt to redirect the social studies from the typical chronological rendering of history, Rugg introduced into that series issues relating to racism, the treatment of immigrants, sexism, efforts to organize labor, inequality in income and living conditions, and government corruption.[16] In time, however, certain business leaders and right-wing groups attacked the books as dangerously socialistic and succeeded in getting at least some school boards to rescind their adoptions. When World War II ended in 1945, American educators heartily embraced life adjustment education, a mixture of educational doctrines dominated by social efficiency.

A Feeble Compromise

Contrary to widespread belief, 20th-century curriculum thinking was not dominated by a two-way struggle between traditionalists, as exemplified in the Committee of Ten report, and a more-or-less unified progressive education movement on the other. Three distinct strains of curriculum thought emerged in the 20th century to challenge the humanistic curriculum that had been dominant in the 19th century. Although proponents of each of these ways of thinking about the curriculum shared a common belief that the traditional academic curriculum was inadequate to the task of modern education, each had quite different reasons for doing so and widely divergent programs for reform. The social efficiency educators saw the traditional curriculum as simply useless except to a small minority of students and urged adoption of a curriculum tied to direct utility and keyed to the probable role that the student would one day occupy. Once the knowledge necessary to function successfully as an adult was determined, that knowledge would become the content of the curriculum. From a social point of view, their vision was of order and stability in a society that seemed in danger of disintegration.

The developmentalist position saw the traditional curriculum as inconsistent with the natural order of development in the child. Their priorities lay with replacing what they regarded as a passive and meaningless approach to schooling with one that appealed directly to the interests of children and their penchant for activity. They envisioned a new curriculum emerging from children's interests and emphasizing active problem solving rather than drill and memorization. Developmentalists consistently regarded the present status of the child as the key to curriculum making, not future adult role.

Finally, the social meliorists saw the traditional curriculum as lacking in social purpose and social concern. Their effort was to rebuild the curriculum around critical social questions affording future citizens the opportunity to grapple with the kinds of problems that society faces. Unlike the social efficiency educators, they did not seek adjustment to the existing society but a new breed of citizens capable of addressing the problems that many believed was a social order urgently needing reconstruction. Each of these forms of curriculum thinking existed alongside the traditional humanistic education, which was also attempting to adapt itself to the demands of modern life. Depending on the social and political climate, each of these approaches made its mark on the American curriculum of today. Neither the traditional curriculum nor any of the three reform movements ever won a clear-cut victory. What passes for the contemporary American curriculum is an agglomeration of all of them.

Since there is no unanimity of opinion at any given time on what is most worthwhile in a culture—whether Aristotle's or ours—it should not be surprising that each of these main currents of curriculum reform would find its adherents. The curriculum, after all, as a selection of elements from the culture reflects to some extent the diversity that exists within the culture. Great value is accorded at one and the same time to mastery of academic subject matter, safe driving, and occupational proficiency as elements in the curriculum. Moreover, social conditions such as the Great Depression and the Cold War created climates that were at least temporarily conducive to different positions at different times. What emerges as a dominant strain in the curriculum is not a function of the force of a particular proposal alone but the due interaction of curriculum ideas and sympathetic or antagonistic social conditions. Therefore, over the course of time, one would expect that first one current then another should assume prominence and that, to some extent, they should all exist side by side.

Moreover, the three currents of curriculum reform must also be seen against the backdrop of a traditional humanist curriculum that consisted of conventional subjects such as English, history, and mathematics. That curriculum proved more resilient than many reformers expected. The substitution of the project for the subject as the basic building block of the curriculum, as followers of Kilpatrick advocated, was too fundamental a change for most to accept, as was the substitution of "areas of living" as some social efficiency educators proposed. Even John Dewey, the quintessential American educational reformer, was, more often than not, interested in reconstructing the existing subjects rather than in replacing them.

Finally, in periods when curriculum reform had charged the atmosphere, it was probably more important for school systems simply to change than to change in a particular ideological direction. Choices at the school level were sometimes politically sensitive or too difficult to implement. At the same time that some proponents of curriculum reform were proclaiming that the curriculum should be derived from the spontaneous interests of children, others were proposing that the curriculum should be a direct and specific preparation for adulthood. Each doctrine had an appeal and a constituency. And, rather than make a particular ideological choice between apparently contradictory curriculum directions, it was perhaps more politically expedient to make a potpourri of all of them.

Notes

[1] Plato, *The Republic*, Book VII (New York: Oxford University Press, 1945. Translated by Francis M. Crawford), p. 244.

[2] Aristotle, *Politics*, Book VIII (London: Oxford at the Clarendon Press, 1946. Translated by Ernest Barker), pp. 333-334.

[3] "Original Papers in Relation to a Course of Liberal Education," *American Journal of Science and Arts* 15 (January 1829): 297-351.

[4] Edward Lee Thorndike and Robert S. Woodworth, "The Influence of Improvement in One Mental Function upon the Efficiency of Other Functions," *Psychological Review* 8, 3 (May 1901): 247-261.

[5] National Education Association, *Cardinal Principles of Secondary Education* (Washington, D.C.: Bureau of Education, 1918).

[6] Charles Francis Adams, *The New Departure in the Common Schools of Quincy and Other Papers on Educational Topics* (Boston: Estes & Lauriat, 1879).

[7] William Heard Kilpatrick, "The Project Method," *Teachers College Record* 19, 4 (September 1918): 319-335.

[8] Albion Small, "Demands of Sociology upon Pedagogy," National Education Association, *Journal of Proceedings and Addresses of the 35th Annual Meeting* (1896): 174.

[9] Ibid.

[10] Ibid., p. 175.

[11] Ibid.

[12] Ibid., p. 180.

[13]Ibid., p. 182.
[14]Ibid., p. 185.
[15]George S. Counts, *Dare the Schools Build a New Social Order?* (New York: John Day and Company, 1932).
[16]See, for example, Harold Rugg, *An Introduction to the Problems of American Culture* (Boston: Ginn and Company, 1931).

Chapter 3. Curriculum Theory/Curriculum Practice: A Gap or The Grand Canyon?

GAIL McCUTCHEON

ITEM: Many principals and teacher educators demand that teachers write behavioral objectives, although curriculum theorists have posed other forms of planning. Further, scholars have critiqued the technical/rational approach to planning because it tends to overfocus on ends at the expense of processes and to emphasize small parts of learning at the expense of a general aim; only certain matters can be attended to that may have little to do with such learnings as creative endeavors. Further, several researchers have found there to be little difference in outcomes, whether a teacher employs or does not employ behavioral objectives;[1] other researchers have found that teachers generally do not think about objectives as a first phase of planning.[2]

ITEM: Many curriculum scholars call for teachers to be involved in curriculum reform, but few teachers report they are vitally interested in it.

ITEM: Probably most teachers across the nation rely heavily on textbooks as the shapers of the curriculum, yet theorists call for teachers to tailor the curriculum to students, local conditions, and currently relevant matters; few curriculum theorists address the matter of textbooks.

Gail McCutcheon is Associate Professor, College of Education, The Ohio State University, Columbus.

Author's note: I wish to acknowledge my brother, John McCutcheon; my colleague, Don Sanders; and Alex Molnar for their careful and helpful comments on an earlier draft of this chapter. A slightly different version was presented at the annual meeting of the Ohio Association for Supervision and Curriculum Development in Columbus in November 1984. Comments and questions from participants were helpful in redrafting.

Clearly, we have a problem in curriculum work. No longer does just a *gap* exist between theory and practice; we currently seem to have a Grand Canyon. This chapter explores some reasons for this phenomenon. Mere understanding of the nature of the problem is, however, not sufficient in my view; action on the part of both academics and practitioners is needed to narrow the gap.

The gap between practice and theory exists for a number of reasons. For example, practitioners and academics alike find maintaining the status quo easier and safer than change. Change requires energy and time, which are often scarce commodities in schools and universities. It also requires a certain level of commitment and security before we can take risks. As humans, we fear the unknown, and the status quo, although perhaps imperfect, is at least safe and known. Further, whether practitioners or academics, we receive few rewards for improving what we do; most of these rewards are intrinsic— recognizing that a student has learned something after quite a struggle, that a research project is beginning to make sense, pride in a job we know is well done. Rarely are rewards extrinsic, such as pay increases or awards for excellence. Hence, there are few extrinsic reasons to improve what we do.

Further, in many ways the culture and structure of schooling works to contain change. For example, administrators, curriculum developers, teachers, parents, and students possess and act upon their own images of what schools are supposed to be; these images may be at odds with those of other practitioners or academics or with what research or theory indicates to be sound. So, the curriculum may be, at least in part, a political artifact as the practitioner strives to appease various groups while realizing his or her own conception of a good curriculum. Moreover, particular policies may tend to conserve the status quo, such as policies on grading, homework, hiring new teachers, student promotions, and the use of textbooks and curriculum guides, as may school routines and other features of a school, such as its architecture or high degree of interest in athletics. Further, hectic school days allow little time for curriculum development, and few schools allocate money for overtime work in this venture.

Academics also contribute to the dilemma of a practice/theory gap by publishing in journals and writing in jargon that renders the work inaccessible to practitioners. Undoubtedly more teachers and administrators read popular magazines than professional journals such as *The Elementary School Journal* or *Theory Into Practice*. Yet it is not considered scholarly, and the promotion, merit pay, and tenure scheme of universities does not reward those who publish in the popular press. While not all work of academics should be published in the popular press, some of it could be. As a result of not writing for teachers and administrators, academics talk to other academics, rather than with practitioners. There has also been, as Schwab characterizes it, a flight from the field—wherein curriculum practice is abandoned for loftier forms of theorizing virtually unusable to many practitioners.[3] Hence, practitioners, who must juggle policies, routines, and competing images of what schools should be, do not commonly consult academics or scholarly articles when reformulating practice, planning something new, or developing theories of action. More often, they turn instead to past experience and other practitioners.[4]

I take the position that theory and research can and should be used by practitioners as they build theories of action. Similarly, classroom experience is crucial if academics are to develop thoughtful and reasonable research projects and theories. Both practitioners and academics possess vital knowledge and experience. A teacher may know all too well how school policies, expectations, or norms affect what can be planned and how certain practices seem to work. Administrators may know how special-interest groups (such as the Moral Majority) influence policies and how to face the practical problems of articulation among various grade and school levels. Academics may know how a particular school is dealing with articulation or curriculum organization or grouping; how another school responded to confrontation between special-interest groups; or ways of gathering information about particular practices, processes of curriculum development, and evaluation. Each group faces particular problems in its work and uses particular resources to treat those problems.

Communication between the groups is necessary to overall curriculum progress. Each group's interpretation can be helpful in shedding light on a problem. The combination of views could be powerful in developing theories grounded in practical realities and in promoting genuine improvement, not merely change. Through collaborative research and curriculum development ventures, this seems feasible.

In this chapter, I will discuss two types of theories: personal theories of action developed by practitioners, and generic theories.

Personal Theories of Action

Teachers' and administrators' theories of action are the set of constructs, beliefs, and principles on which practitioners base decisions and actions. Practitioners develop these theories through their experiences and reflections, and to a lesser extent through reading or hearing about generic theory. Such theories illuminate and guide practitioners' work because they comprise interrelated sets of interpretations about what should be taught and learned, how to improve and evaluate teaching and learning, and how to deal with daily tasks of managing curriculum development, classes, and work. Administrators also develop such action theories to guide their support of teachers' instructional improvement and curriculum development, and school management.[5]

Parts of practitioners' theories may be tacit; if asked, they might not be able to express fully what they believe. Action is no less valid based on such tacit theories, however. Each day practitioners face a host of complex, context-specific problems about which there are no easy, certain answers. No singular "right" course of action is available, although practitioners can envision certain courses as better than others. In facing these problems, they *must* take action. Underlying these actions is a personal, guiding theory. By pausing to reflect, by reaching inward and attempting to understand that personal theory of action, teachers and administrators exercise the most professional aspect of practice. By analyzing students' written assignments, oral responses, and activities, teachers can determine whether particular courses of action work well.

The study of teaching practice has unfortunately, in recent years, been conducted by outsiders. Perhaps due to the press of time, practitioners may notice bored faces or an increase in discipline problems, but they seldom research their own work in order to improve it.

If developing oral language skills is important, for example, a history teacher could arrange small group work to plan and paint murals about important events in the Industrial Revolution, then could listen to the groups at work, tape record group discussions, and interview the students to discern the effectiveness of the assignment. In order to improve one's practice and professionalism such inquiry is necessary. Through such inquiry in *this* context with *these* students and *this* subject matter, we come to know our own methods, their effectiveness, and how they might be improved, according to the practitioner's criteria. This does not happen through statewide mandates revising the course-work needed for certification, nor through adoption of a new text series, nor through the development of a curriculum guide. It happens individually as we develop, grow, and learn about our practice by becoming students of it.

This sort of endeavor, at the heart of professional practice, can be supported in several ways. In faculty meetings, teachers could relate their inquiry to others, to begin to develop a common lore and understanding of practice. For example, after school one day, a group of teachers of 13- and 14-year-olds recently discussed with me and each other how they allowed students to change a certain assignment to make it more realistic or personally relevant. In literature, for instance, students assigned to read the same novel conceived of their own questions to answer about the work. The teacher either approved or met with students to reconceive the questions. The literature teacher remarked that most of the student-generated questions were much more difficult than ones she would have asked. In home economics, students planned their own apartments, which called for skills of measurement as well as design. Students decided individually the dimensions of the apartment and how many rooms it had, then determined a realistic decorating budget with the teacher. Mathematics, science, and technology teachers discussed lessons where students had some role in formulating the task. Students reported that their own tasks were more challenging and less boring than ones set totally by teachers. Teachers reported more work, a higher quality of work, and more interest on the part of students. By collecting evidence of the value of such negotiable tasks, teachers increased their understanding of their importance to students and planned to include more of them through the year.

Sharing such research can be helpful in establishing a climate conducive to inquiry into one's professional life. Another way of supporting it is through ties with other professionals. Undoubtedly, an outsider, a colleague, or an academic collaborating on a project with the practitioner is of great value in this enterprise, for by describing practice and talking about why a certain action is taken, the teacher or administrator can begin to understand his or her action theory. Talking about theory permits people to examine those theories they hold and, eventually, this leads to a fuller understanding, a possession of one's own theory. Through language, then, we come to know our teaching selves. Reading theoretical work and research studies may also help practitioners to develop and understand their theories of action. Faced with other ideas, practitioners can compare views and gain an understanding or expand their own theory after this comparison. In this fashion, discussions of practice in faculty meetings, teachers' lounges, seminars, coursework, observing colleagues, or reading about theory and practice may assist with the endeavor of understanding one's theory of action.

Many practitioners probably hold similar theories, and as we begin to discuss them professionally, theories may develop that will be useful to the field as a whole. Further, we may enhance the feeling of belonging to a community of education.

Generic Theories of Action

A difficulty some cite with developing generic theories about education is that contexts vary so greatly: people differ from one setting to the next, requirements for graduation vary, curriculum may be different, as may other matters. The dilemma is, how can we generalize about different phenomena? Others argue that fundamental commonalities exist, and hence we *can* generalize about those matters. Like personal theories of action, generic theories can also guide and illuminate practice by pointing to alternatives. For example, Eisner and Vallance describe five competing orientations to what could be taught and learned.[6] Tyler (1949) describes a technical, rational way to plan a curriculum,[7] and Reid describes a deliberate approach.[8] Assumptions underlying the orientations and their justifications as described and exemplified in Eisner and Vallance's book are in conflict, as are the conflicts between Tyler's and Reid's assumptions underlying curriculum planning. Practitioners who read such literature can mull over the literature and compare it to their practice. However, if generic theories are to be useful in illuminating or calling into question our personal theories of action, they must be readable—and few generic theories are.

Similarly, personal theories can influence academics' attempts at developing generic theory. Now, this may be rather idealistic, for in truth, few academics observe, do research, or talk with practitioners sufficiently to understand their personal theories. Since many facets of the action theory are probably tacit—not held at a level of conscious awareness—this would be a time-consuming endeavor. Further, few teachers see it within their role to publish research about their own practice or their personal theories. Lacking such communication, it is not difficult to understand why the gap between theory and practice has widened. Rather than working to inform one another's views, we work apart. This is unfortunate, and it is difficult to see how curriculum can solve its problems without open communication between practitioners and academics.

A Call For Action

I believe we could take several courses of action to narrow the gap between theory and practice. Clearly it is time for us to act responsibly to shape the field of curriculum, for academics and practitioners can offer one another a great deal in facing the problems that confront us—problems of what to teach; how to organize it; how to engender continuity, integration, and coherence in the curriculum; how to discern what is being learned in classrooms; how to write materials that people can and will use; how to develop theories that are appropriate and significant in facilitating our understanding of curriculum matters. One problem with this view is that practitioners and academics may have little influence over the curriculum destiny; it may rest in the hands of state departments of education, textbook publishers, and special-interest groups—all the more reason for academics and practitioners to join forces.

What sorts of activities could we engage in to open communication? For one, practitioners and academics could work collaboratively on jointly defined problems. This work would be helpful to practitioners by creating a situation that would support their own elaboration and understanding of their theories of action. Collaboration would also increase their sense of professionalism, of belonging to the enterprise of curriculum work. And it would facilitate learning research skills which could be useful in other situations as well, for example, documenting what students are learning, the difficulties students encounter with a particular subject, and so forth. Academics would benefit from the experience by understanding more fully the nature of practice and the sorts of problems teachers and administrators face, as well as what they consider important and influential. As a result, we could develop grounded, practical theories to help us understand such matters as the context of teaching, its problematic and tentative nature, and the mix of values and ideas about what is important to include in the curriculum.[8]

This implies discarding our beliefs that the Other Side (if we're academics—practitioners; if we're practitioners—academics) cannot be trusted or is ineffective. It further implies that we must treat one another as equals—experts in different matters. It also implies that practitioners must learn research skills, and that we must believe in the power of individuals to improve education rather than relying heavily on top-down, bureaucratic notions of effectiveness. Such notions strip away dispositions necessary to developing a profession of education. Professional responsibility and control are removed when someone remote from the classroom issues a mandate, a "teacher-proof" set of curriculum materials or examinations. There is no need to reflect, only to follow a set of instructions, more like a technician (such as a plumber or telephone repairer) than a professional.

Finally, we need to develop feelings of genuine responsibility to one another to provide and to ask for information, guidance, criticism, and other forms of assistance to improve the nature of schools, the curriculum of schools and colleges, and the writing about them. We must develop a concerted, collaborative effort in this enterprise if we are to succeed.

Another potentially fruitful course of action would be the development of local groups to deliberate about site-specific curriculum matters. The groups could draw from several school systems and colleges, and work as a task force to resolve a school-related problem common to several sites, such as a need for curriculum development. In these times of scarce financial resources, and when many recent reports have implications for curriculum reform, it may be prudent to share the resources and responsibilities necessary to such work. Through listening to others articulate their views, individuals within the group may reach a common understanding and appreciation. Clearly, if we are to progress, teachers, administrators, and academics must learn to work collegially to resolve dilemmas and to carry out research that has a potential for being useful.

Finally, with the surfacing of so many reports—at times conflicting—it seems appropriate for us to reassess matters, to take actions aimed at improving schools. Because various people have different expertise and perspectives, and because the difficulties we face are complex and rarely have clear or easy solutions, collaboration is likely to be a fruitful course of action.

Notes

[1]See, for example, Philippe C. Duchastel and Paul F. Merrill, "The Effects of Behavioral Objectives on Learning: A Review of Empirical Studies," *Review of Educational Research* 43, 1 (1973): 53-69.

[2]See, for example, Gail McCutcheon, "Elementary School Teachers' Planning for Social Studies and Other Subjects," *Theory and Research in Social Education* 9, 1 (1981): 45-66.

[3]Joseph J. Schwab, "The Practical: A Language for Curriculum," *School Review* 78 (1969): 1-24.

[4]Dan C. Lortie, *Schoolteacher* (Chicago: University of Chicago Press, 1975).

[5]See Carr and S. Kemmis, *Becoming Critical: Knowing Through Action Research* (Victoria: Deakin University Press, 1983); and Donald P. Sanders and Gail McCutcheon, "On the Evolution of Teachers' Theories of Action Through Action Research," presented at the annual conference of the American Educational Research Association, New Orleans, April 1984.

[6]Elliot W. Eisner and Elizabeth Vallance, eds., *Conflicting Conceptions of Curriculum* (Berkeley: McCutchan, 1974).

[7]Ralph Tyler, *Basic Principles of Curriculum and Instruction* (Chicago: University of Chicago Press, 1949).

[8]William A. Reid, *Thinking About the Curriculum* (London: Routledge and Kegan Paul, 1978).

Chapter 4. Psychological Theory and Curricular Thinking

BERNICE J. WOLFSON

In the study of psychological theory, we hope to find valuable guidelines to enhance our thinking and, ultimately, the way we design curriculums. I do not think, however, that psychological theory directly influences curricular thinking. Rather, psychological theory, both tacit and explicit, *indirectly interacts* with our curricular thinking and curriculum practice.

In using the word "theory," I select the meaning that is most compatible with my perspective, one suggested by theoretical physicist David Bohm:

> ... a theory is primarily a form of *insight*, i.e. a way of looking at the world, and not a form of *knowledge* of how the world is ... all theories are insights, which are neither true nor false but, rather, clear in certain domains, and unclear when extended beyond these domains. ... When we look at the world through our theoretical insights, the factual knowledge that we obtain will evidently be shaped and formed by our theories.[1]

Thus our psychological theories are the "tinted glasses," part of the personal perspective through which we create and explain our world, including such concepts as teaching and learning, human behavior, and thinking. In this sense every person selects and constructs psychological theory from his or her educational and other experiences in the world. We are continuously (whether unconsciously or consciously) testing our insights in action and

Bernice J. Wolfson is Professor of Education, University of Alabama at Birmingham.

testing our action for congruence with our insights. For example, teachers often say, based on behaviorist insights, that reward promotes learning. Their tinted glasses help them see this happen in their classrooms. Thus theory supports our way of perceiving and acting in the world. We may choose to test our insights by empirical studies, by reasoning, or by reflecting on our experience. We will modify our theories as we are open to new experiences. Our theories and experiences are interactive; each colors the other—with the possibility of creating new perspectives and actions.

What psychological theory does not provide, however, is knowledge and principles that can be *applied* to and, therefore, directly influence curriculum thinking and teaching.

In 1892 William James made a similar point (though with a different reason):

> I say moreover that you make a great, a very great mistake, if you think that psychology, being a science of the mind's laws, is something from which you can deduce definite programmes and schemes and methods of instruction for immediate schoolroom use. Psychology is a science, and teaching is an art; and sciences never generate arts directly out of themselves. An intermediary inventive mind must make the application, by using its originality ... the teaching must *agree* with psychology, but must not necessarily be the only kind of teaching that would agree; for many diverse methods of teaching may equally well agree with psychological laws.[2]

However, we have no general agreement about *psychological laws*. There are many diverse psychological theories. It should follow that different ways of thinking about psychology may be congruent with different ways of thinking about curriculum.

Today, curriculum designs and decisions are made by state legislators and state boards of education, by consultants and editors for textbook companies and local school systems, and by classroom teachers and college professors. People who make these decisions ask a variety of questions: What should go on in schools with children of various ages? What sequences of content are desirable? How shall we "package" resources? How shall we organize teaching and learning? No doubt they also think about the learning process and instructional procedures, theories of child development, societal demands, and so forth. What each of these people accepts, both explicitly and tacitly, about the nature of learning (psychological insights) and what should be learned (philosophical and sociological insights) necessarily helps shape how each thinks about and plans curriculum.

To uncover the relationship between psychological theory and curricular thinking, I will first describe briefly three prominent theoretical orientations in psychology and give examples of curricular thinking consistent with these orientations. Each orientation may be seen as a different set of colored glasses; the questions the psychologists ask, the concepts they create, and the facts they identify are constrained by their insights. Their theories are not to be judged as correct or incorrect, but as helpful or unhelpful in answering the questions we ask. The reader should keep in mind that psychologists of different orientations have pursued different purposes, focused on different aspects of human activity, and developed different concepts as part of their theories.

The three psychological orientations that I shall discuss are behavioral, developmental (cognitive), and phenomenological. These are not discrete categories, and within each orientation there are numerous viewpoints. Therefore my descriptions should be seen as loosely representing each orientation.

Behavioral Psychology

Behavioral psychologists developed concepts such as associationism, connectionism, classical conditioning, and instrumental conditioning to explain how the environment can be planned to produce desired behavior. Psychologists in this category include, among others, R.M. Gagne, D.O. Hebb, and B.F. Skinner.[3]

Insights from behavioral psychology which are often reflected in the work of curriculum planners include:

1. Reward, or immediate feedback, is necessary for learning to occur.

2. Learning proceeds by building from simple behaviors to more complex combinations of behavior.

3. Learning tasks should be presented in an ordered sequence.

4. Skills are hierarchical.

5. Desired performance should be specified in advance.

6. Repetition and practice are important to produce learning.[4]

A behavioristic perspective is congruent with curriculum planning which emphasizes specifying behavioral objectives for the learner and providing content in small, simple units which must be learned as a basis for learning larger or more complicated units.[5]

Behaviorism has been criticized as inadequate to account for both complex human behavior and thinking, and the social and emotional aspects of human beings.[6] Nevertheless, many behavioristic concepts such as the use of rewards and the need for practice are part of our culture.

Developmental Psychology

Psychologists have also studied how human beings develop. Some psychologists, such as Gesell[7] and Bayley,[8] have been concerned with describing normal patterns of growth. Cognitive psychologists, such as Piaget, Bruner, Luria, and Vygotsky[9] were interested in the development of children's thinking and the relationship between thinking and language. Psycholinguists such as Smith and Goodman[10] can also be considered to have a cognitive orientation, having studied the nature and development of language and of the reading process.

Developmental concepts from the psychoanalytic theories of Freud and Erikson,[11] such as ego, stages of development, and unconscious motivation, have become part of our language and our culture. Students of early childhood education in particular have paid attention to psychoanalytic insights. Other developmental psychologists have focused on specific stages of development such as infancy and adolescence. Thus it hardly seems surprising to find the concepts of maturation and developmental stages frequently noted in curriculum designs.

Developmental cognitive psychologists have studied the development and function of the mind. Their theories have been variously described by the terms Gestalt/field theory, developmentalism, structuralism, and constructivism. Essentially, these psychologists study how the mind functions as inferred from verbal or motoric responses, perception of the environment, problem solving, and development of language and thinking. Their theories are of interest to curriculum developers concerned with how we should support the development of infants and young children.

Some common insights congruent with various cognitive theories, which may be familiar to curricular thinkers, include:

1. Children are active, purposive agents in their own learning and development.

2. Children develop cognitive structures (processes, schemata, networks) as a result of interaction of self and environment.

3. Structural development is related to age and cultural contexts.[12]

4. Education should be aimed at providing opportunities to develop new understandings and insights.[13]

5. Acting transforms thinking and thinking transforms action.

6. The interests of children are important in the learning process.

Cognitive psychological perspectives are consonant with curriculum planning which takes into account the developmental level and interests of the child and which seeks to provide for active involvement of children in school learning.

A limitation of cognitive theory is that it, too, is not helpful when we try to understand how emotional and social aspects of human development and learning relate to cognitive development.

Phenomenological Psychology

Phenomenological psychologists focus on discovery of the individual's unique perceptions, awareness, choices, and holistic development, as a person in the world, a point of view similar to that of humanistic and existential psychologists. These psychologists construe human beings as active, purposive, feeling, thinking persons, moving toward self-actualization, transforming their environment and, at the same time, being transformed by it.[14]

Some phenomenological insights which may be accepted by curricular thinkers include:

1. Each student's unique perspective is significant for learning.
2. Knowledge is personally constructed, but socially shared.
3. Any system of knowledge is a way of interpreting the world.
4. An individual makes decisions on the basis of his or her perceptions.
5. No matter how the curriculum is designed, learners create their own meanings.
6. Individuals develop self-concepts, that is, one's perception of self emerges in interaction with other people in a cultural context.
7. Students' self-concept is an important factor in their ability to learn.
8. Students and teachers pursue self-actualization in social contexts.

A phenomenological perspective is most likely to be expressed in process terms; communicating and creating personal meaning are considered paramount. Sharing personal perspectives serves to increase awareness of other people's perspectives and of the multiplicity of viewpoints in the world. Persons are viewed as active in constructing their world and in making choices. Curriculum emerges from personal interests and biographical experiences in interaction with the cultural setting. Curriculum is seen to be a matter of possibilities.[15]

A limitation of this perspective, as seen by psychologists of other persuasions, is that it is not scientific in that its propositions are not supported by a series of rigorous empirical studies.[16]

How Do Psychological Insights Enter the Curriculum?

We all have psychological beliefs. Explicitly or implicitly all educators have assumptions about what people are like and how they develop. We also have assumptions about how learning occurs and why people are motivated to learn.

Since most undergraduate and graduate programs in teacher education have, for at least the last 40 years, included some study of psychology, it is likely that most teachers and curriculum workers participated in discussions of psychological concepts. In such classes, educators encounter a varied range of concepts depending on the course focus, the textbook used, and the knowledge and experience of the instructor. In addition, what is learned is related to the students' previous knowledge and experience.

What has this exposure to psychology meant to teachers and curriculum workers? Explicitly, perhaps not very much. Education students often question the usefulness of such courses, but this does not preclude their incorporating new ideas into their framework of thought. When we study and agree with some particular psychological theory, in the very process of accepting and integrating those values and modifying our programs or practices, we *neces-sarily* interpret and modify that theory as a result of our unique history, experiences, and understandings. We *construct* our own perspective. This perspective will enter into our choices as we carry out the task of curriculum making.

As formal curriculum decisions are made—for example, a curriculum guide for a school system, a textbook for a course, or a new approach to teaching math—some attention is usually given to certain psychological concepts. Most likely the developmental level of the students and beliefs about the nature of human learning and motivation will be considered. When we think about designing curriculum, it *does* make a difference whether we assume that people learn because they are rewarded or because it is a natural part of life. It *does* make a difference whether we assume that what people think and feel are essential aspects of learning, or that the "right" responses are our only concern.

It is my perception that the most commonly held insights in our schools today are those of behavioristic psychology. This perspective is especially noticeable in special education curricular thinking. There is, however, a growing emphasis on cognitive studies. Some educators have attempted to plan and implement programs consistent with the theories of Piaget[17] and Bruner.[18] There are also humanistic or phenomenological thinkers who reject behavioristic assumptions and the curriculum practices related to those assumptions.[19]

The Interaction Between Psychological Theory and Curricular Thinking

Curricular thinking occurs in many different settings, is initiated in a variety of ways, and involves many different types of participants. I shall discuss how Jerome Bruner, a cognitive psychologist, and Carl Rogers, a humanistic or phenomenological psychologist, have involved themselves in curricular thinking and implementation. Their work in education illustrates that psychological insights are not the only insights that enter into their curricular thinking, and that these insights were not *directly applied*. I shall also describe how psycholinguistic theory, as used by Frank Smith and Kenneth Goodman, enters into curricular thinking and practice.

A Cognitive Curriculum

Bruner describes himself as a "wandering intellectual."[20] Experimentation, teaching, and writing are his way of life. He defines himself as a "rationalist, structuralist and intuitionist."[21]

In studying the development of humankind, Bruner concluded that "man could not have made that voyage without the aid of the ready-made tools of a culture and its language, that mental growth comes as much from the outside in as from the inside out."[22]

To Bruner, the object of education is to "penetrate a subject, not to cover it. You do this by 'spiraling' into it: a first pass to get the intuitive sense of it, later passes over the same domain go into it more deeply and more fully."[23]

Bruner's curriculum experiences centered around the development and testing of a social studies curriculum, *Man: A Course of Study* (1965), designed for 4th to 6th graders. His colleagues in this enterprise included "anthropologists, zoologists, linguists, theoretical engineers, artists, designers, camera crews, teachers, children and psychologists."[24]

The content of this course is the nature of man and "the forces that shape his humanity."[25] The three questions that recur throughout the course are: "What is human about human beings? How did they get that way? How can they be made more so?"[26] Bruner wrote:

We had high aspirations. We hoped to achieve five goals:
1. To give our pupils respect for and confidence in the powers of their own minds.

2. To give them respect, moreover, for the powers of thought concerning the human condition, man's plight, and his social life.

3. To provide them with a set of workable models that make it simpler to analyze the nature of the social world in which they live and the condition in which man finds himself.

4. To impart a sense of respect for the capacities and plight of man as a species, for his origins, for his potential, for his humanity.

5. To leave the student with a sense of the unfinished business of man's evolution.[27]

These goals are different from those that would have been written by a behaviorist. Bruner's goals are cognitive and attitudinal; a behaviorist would specify performance objectives. A phenomenologist most likely would not start out with specific goals. Bruner's goals, in fact, don't seem to be explicitly related to his psychological theories, nor need they be. What is implicit are his psychological insights about the nature of human beings. Many of these goals also reflect the personal values of Bruner and the other participants who planned with him. But since this course was developed with a large group of consultants, it would be impossible for an outsider to know how these goals were selected. What is important to recognize is that psychological insights did not entirely nor directly define the goals of *Man: A Course of Study*.

Most educators are familiar to some extent with this course, the excitement it engendered in participants, and its subsequent rejection by most public schools—due in part to political opposition by groups who considered the discussion of certain ideas inappropriate in the schools. This rejection illustrates how out-of-school factors limit the psychological and curricular ideas allowed in schools. Bruner wrote:

> The paramount virtue of the course, as one teacher put it to me, was that it posed problems in such a way that teacher and student both knew that they were together at the frontier of their thinking, brooding about the nature of man. If I did not know at the start, I certainly know now that you cannot address that question in school without plunging into the central political issue of education.[28]

While Bruner's insights about cognitive development[29] may be familiar to curriculum workers, those workers rarely follow his approach to curriculum development and implementation. In the final analysis, developing curriculum *a àla* Bruner would radically change what goes on in most schools. Students would be more actively engaged; reflection, discussion, and inquiry would be frequent; and curriculum plans and materials would be developed by groups representing various experts and constituencies. While the main purpose of a Bruner curriculum would be the development of the mind, he would also include the arts, which he believes give meaning to the human predicament. Curriculums such as Bruner's would require a major commitment of time educators' production of materials for students and teachers, and additional education for teachers. Bruner believes that today's schools do not engage the active thinking of children and thus contribute to the problem of education, not the solution.

A Humanistic Curriculum

Carl Rogers, a humanistic psychologist, came to education by way of counseling. His approach to education is person-centered. His view is that:

> ... in a genuinely human climate, which the teacher can initiate, a young person can find him or herself respected, can make responsible choices, can experience the excitement of learning, can lay the basis for living as an effective concerned citizen, well informed, competent in knowledge and skills, confident in facing the future.[30]

In his book, *Freedom To Learn for the 80's*, Rogers reports the work of a number of teachers at all levels of education who have been moved to change the way they work with students as a result of reading his work or participating in his workshops. He also reports research in the United States and Germany which tests the effectiveness of his conception of teaching for the development of human potential.

In describing the goals of education in his book, Rogers states:

> It aims toward a climate of trust in the classroom in which curiosity and the natural desire to learn can be nourished and enhanced ... a participatory mode of decision-making in all aspects of learning in which students, teachers, and administrators each have a part ... helping students to prize themselves, to build their confidence and self-esteem ... uncovering the excitement in intellectual and emotional discovery, which leads students to become life-long learners ... helping teachers to grow as persons, finding rich satisfaction in their interaction with learners.—Even more deeply, it aims toward an awareness that, for all of us, the good life is within, not something which is dependent on outside sources.[31]

While Bruner's curricular goals reflect a desire to develop students' thinking (a focus of some of his psychological work) and attitudes in relation to specific content, Rogers' goals are broadly stated to include the total context of the student-teacher-environment and the self-actualization of persons in the educational setting. Rogers regards mental development as *inseparable* from other aspects of human development. He emphasizes that "significant learning combines the logical *and* the intuitive, the intellect *and* the feelings, the concept *and* the experience, the idea *and* the meaning."[32]

Rogers believes that the "... primary task of the teacher is to *permit* the student to learn, to feed his or her own curiosity. Merely to absorb facts is only of slight value in the present, and usually of less value in the future. Learning *how* to learn is the element that is always of value, now and in the future. Thus the teacher's task is delicate, demanding and a truly exalted calling."[33] From his point of view teaching changes to the "facilitation of learning," and Rogers explores how a facilitator enables students to learn or become, a concept closely tied to his insights about human beings.

The essential qualities of a facilitator include genuineness, prizing, and empathy. Rogers discusses the meaning of these qualities and how a teacher might become a more humanistic, student-centered facilitator. There are no blueprints, since each facilitator is unique, as are the context and the students in the class. In fact, the students and the facilitator are the ultimate curriculum makers.

In looking at the classroom, and how curriculum decisions are made there, Rogers differentiates between the role of a facilitator and that of a traditional teacher: "... the *good* traditional teacher asks her or himself questions of this sort: 'What do I think would be good for a student to learn at this particular age and level of competence? How can I plan a proper curriculum for this student? How can I inculcate motivation to learn this curriculum? How can I instruct in such a way that he or she will gain the knowledge that should be gained? How can I best set an examination to see whether this knowledge has actually been taken in?'"[34] While these questions may not be asked by *every* good traditional teacher, they show that teachers typically expect to make curriculum and practical decisions for their students, based on prior curriculum decisions, judgments about what should be learned, and their own beliefs about children and learning.

By contrast, Rogers' facilitator is first asking questions of the students: "What do you want to learn? What things puzzle you? What problems do you wish you could solve?" Guided by the students' answers, the facilitator asks him- or herself:

"Now how can I help him or her find the resources—the people, the experience, the learning facilities, the books, the knowledge in myself—that will help them learn in ways that will provide answers to the things that concern them, the things they are eager to learn?" Also "How can I help them evaluate their own progress and set future learning goals based on this self-evaluation?"[35]

Developing curriculum *à la* Rogers would entail a large measure of decision making by students—freedom with responsibility. Although the general area of a course, and some requirements as well, may be defined by the facilitator or the curriculum guide, the curriculum which *emerges* will be the result of interaction between teacher, students, and selected content. It is likely to have more variety than usually occurs when final curriculum decisions are made by the program or the teacher. The students would be active in searching, planning, and discussing, and also in the creation of appropriate products.

Although the psychological insights of Rogers and Bruner differ—they ask different questions, focus on different domains, and approach curriculum thinking differently—both Bruner and Rogers are concerned about the need for educating thoughtful, self-directed, responsible, and compassionate students so that the problems of the world may be solved better by the next generation. Either approach to curriculum planning, if widely used, would revolutionize our schools and possibly our society. However, introduction of their programs has aroused conservative opposition and political attacks by supporters of the status quo.[36]

A Psycholinguistic Foundation

Many other curriculum programs have been designed for the teaching of various school subjects, such as math, science, reading, and, now, computer literacy. These programs are initiated by textbook companies, subject matter specialists and educators with government grants, or by independent educational organizations. A variety of consultants are usually involved in this curriculum making. Frequently, some psychological concepts or theories are stated as part of the rationale for the design. For example, the writers of the Science Curriculum Improvement Study (SCIS) Grades K-6 (1970), developed at the University of California, Berkeley, discussed Piaget's work as the psychological foundation of their curriculum design.[37]

In another curriculum area, the teaching of reading, psycholinguistic theorists such as Frank Smith and Kenneth Goodman have developed new insights about the reading process which are significant for curricular thinking. Their conclusions, combined with those of other researchers who closely observed children engaged in reading, such as Y. Goodman, Clark, and Clay,[38] have led to a new conception of the reading process. Consequently, some curriculum workers and teachers have reexamined their insights about reading and *how* they can best help children to become readers.

This new research suggests that reading is a single (holistic) process. The act of reading is focused on meaning and involves predicting and verifying the text using, simultaneously and interdependently, three cuing systems:

semantics (including knowledge of the world as well as meaning in the text), syntax, and the graphophonic system.[39]

We now have to ask what sort of curriculum planning and implementation would be congruent with this conception of the reading process. Smith wrote that "reading cannot be formally taught, that children learn to read only by reading, but that provided children have adequate opportunity to explore and test their hypotheses in a world of meaningful print, they can and do succeed in learning to read."[40] Smith went on to point out that the teacher has a critical role in helping children learn to read and that teachers who understand the reading process and have a sensitive awareness of the feelings, interests, and abilities of their students are best equipped to assist children as they progress in reading. He emphasized, however, that "learning to read can be perceived as making sense of more and more kinds of language in more contexts, fundamentally a matter of experience."[41]

This psycholinguistic perspective (which is also congruent with many cognitive and phenomenological insights) is consistent with a curriculum plan that makes use of the language experience approach to early reading (that is, using children's own language for beginning reading) and that provides many opportunities for children to use oral and written language in meaningful contexts. Children are viewed as active in making sense of the reading process. They learn the alphabet and sound symbol relationships *as they read*. This perspective rejects separate skill activities and fragmentation of the reading process as meaningless to the child and not helpful in becoming a reader.

However, the concept of reading which predominates in today's schools is consistent with behavioristic psychology and assumes a process of learning to read by recognizing sound-symbol relationships (phonics), putting sounds together to make words and words together to make sentences. Meaning, or comprehension, is the end product desired. From this framework curriculum workers have designed programs in which children are taught the alphabet, the sounds of letters, simple words, and then simplified text (Run, Spot, run.) followed by more complex words, paragraphs, and longer texts. Children are taught "word recognition skills" such as sounding out letters and blending the sounds into words, structural analysis, comprehension skills, and study skills. Usually a continuum of skills is designed for kindergarten through 6th grade.

This predominant interpretation of the reading process, as recommended in reading textbooks, is congruent with the following behavioristic insights: There is a best sequence for learning; children should be rewarded for correct answers; teacher- or textbook-planned activities should be built according to the best sequence; time must be spent practicing the skills and, of course, evaluating whether or not children have learned them.

I believe it makes a difference which psychological insights we hold about the reading process (or about doing math or science) and about how people learn. Such insights will become part of our thinking about how to help children learn in school. The current emphasis on testing puts constraints on curriculum decisions that are particularly obvious in the reading curriculum. Since tests are usually based on a skills approach (congruent with behavioristic insights), it is difficult for teachers to emphasize a whole-language approach which is congruent with psycholinguistic insights. Also, most textbooks and their accompanying workbooks assume the necessity of learning a sequence of isolated skills.

In practice, however, teachers tend to be eclectic, having selectively integrated various philosophical, psychological, and practical beliefs (some of which may appear to be incompatible) into their individual perspectives. Thus, in carrying out their reading programs, some teachers incorporate children's literature, a language-experience approach, recreational reading and other language-arts experiences. Many textbooks also recommend a wide range of activities in addition to skills activities. There is, nevertheless, a basic contradiction between the two main explanations of the reading process. Fortunately, most children succeed in constructing the reading process themselves.

These various examples illustrate that curricular thinking usually includes explicit or implicit psychological insights. These insights interact (along with other insights and values) in some indeterminate fashion with the processes of curricular thinking and planning.

Insights for the Future

Society is continually changing. As Luria has demonstrated, marked social change is accompanied by changes in the structure of mental processes. His research led him to conclude: "sociohistoric shifts not only introduce new content into the mental world of human beings; they also create new forms of activity and new structures of cognitive functioning. They advance human consciousness to new levels."[42]

New events and trends in society will greatly change our world[43] and affect how we think and feel. Over time, from these events and our own changes, new insights about human beings will emerge and will enter into the thinking of curriculum makers. I shall mention just three areas of change that are especially significant for psychological insights and curricular thinking now and in the future.

1. *The development of computers.* It will affect our lives in basic ways. It is not clear how television has changed us and our view of the world; but no one doubts that it has. Growing up with computers will surely modify, or even radically change, the way human beings *experience* the world.[44] Our insights into development and learning will also inevitably change.

While our understanding of these changes is probably a long way off, as we think about curriculum we need to be alert to what this new event in our world may mean. If learning is seen as acquiring information, how should we use computers in schools? However, if learning is seen as a matter of sharing and negotiating meaning, what educational purposes can computers serve? What changes will we see in the social development of young children avidly using computers? Can we determine the desirable uses of computers in schools?[45] Are we using computers as electronic workbook pages? Will schools become overcommitted to technological thinking? Who is studying these questions from a psychological and sociological perspective?

2. *The women's movement.* Psychologists, mostly female, have begun to rethink the insights of psychology about child development and human characteristics.[46] Can we change our perceptions of human nature to include women equally with men? Can we integrate the history of women into the history men have developed, where women are invisible? Both the American Psychological Association and the American Educational Research Association have sizable groups concerned with such issues, as well as issues of equity in curriculum plans and in work opportunities. Will their new insights become part of the curriculum thinker's perspective?[47]

3. *The brain and the mind.* There are many new insights about how the brain works, growing out of physiological and neurological research and the work of cognitive psychologists and psycholinguists. At the same time there are many questions still to be answered. What do we mean by *mind*? How does that concept relate to the brain?[48] As studies continue, new insights will have significance for curricular thinking. (There will be, unfortunately, many misinterpretations of the meaning of these insights, for example, the interpretation of what left brain-right brain differences mean for school curriculum.[49])

Our thinking about curriculum will constantly be challenged by new ideas, experiences, and political change. Psychology will provide only a small part of the insights each of us will use as we carry out our curricular thinking. When we negotiate curriculum decisions we can share our perspectives and expand our awareness—even transform our viewpoints—and, thus, our thinking about curriculum.

Personal Experiences

When I was asked to write this chapter, it seemed so right. I had thought and taught about these matters for about 25 years. I had also taught high school and elementary school. Here seemed to be a great opportunity to synthesize my knowledge and experience. But now that I have completed most of the chapter, I must admit I am dissatisfied. As Polanyi has pointed out "... nothing that is said, written or printed, can ever mean anything in itself: for it is only a *person* who utters something—or who listens to it or reads it—who can mean something by it...."[50] Thus, I want to describe some of my own experiences that brought me to my present perceptions in order to illustrate how one person experienced the interaction between psychological insights, curricular thinking, and practice.

Socialized to be a "good student," I tried to satisfy the teacher, although often I couldn't figure out what answer she wanted. Throughout elementary school and high school I assumed that knowledge was "out there," unchangeable, and that it was my job to ingest it. A few teachers stand out in my memory as apparently interested in students and interesting to me.

A large amount of my out-of-school time was spent reading. I was curious about how other people lived, what they thought about, and how they felt. Books were an endless and continuous source of vicarious experience and real meaning.

At college I was amazed at how much more there was to learn than I had dreamed of: anthropology, philosophy, psychology, and much more. Although the content of learning was mostly what had been written by others, what I would call developed knowledge, I became aware that I was trying to connect these meanings with what I already knew and also to reflect on what it all meant to me. In completing my B.A. degree I took my first educational psychology course and was certified to teach English and social studies in high school.

When I started to teach at a vocational high school, I was confronted with questions I had not faced before: How could I communicate meaningfully with my students? What knowledge might have meaning to them? How could I maintain a reasonably orderly classroom? There was a lot about how boys act in groups that I didn't understand. How could I obtain cooperation? My main concern was to plan lessons that might touch the lives of the boys in my classes. I probably succeeded in reaching fewer than half the boys some of the time. I experimented with many approaches. I survived. And I learned more about myself, the students, and schools. Perhaps what was most interesting and significant was the experience itself: meeting 35 boys each period, most of whom were bigger than I; boys of varied ethnic and social backgrounds whose life experiences were very different from mine. I was trying to involve them in material such as Mark Twain, American history, and current events.

My next educational experience was teaching modern dance in college. In three years I turned my approach upside down. From directing all the class activity, I changed to presenting problems for students to work out singly or in small groups. Students, I found, could work best from their individual natural movement, style, and tempo to extend their movement range and performance.

Then, in teaching elementary school I struggled with some of the same questions I had when teaching high school, but in a new context. I reexperienced some of the same insights, as well as new ones. It took me a while to understand the children in my classes, in spite of child-development courses. It took me three years to learn that I could be myself in the classroom, rather than acting the way I thought a teacher was expected to act. At the same time I was doing graduate work in educational psychology. This work did not seem very helpful in the classroom until I read Snygg and Combs.[51]

Again, when I taught educational psychology and elementary school curriculum in college, I relearned some of the same lessons. I moved from lecturing, giving assignments, and asking questions to seeking active involvement and thinking by students; encouraging students to express their ideas and to hear the ideas of others; and suggesting activities and problems for students to work out individually and in small groups. I became certain that transmitting developed knowledge is not enough. What is most important is thinking about knowledge and experience and constructing personal meaning. Indeed this process, it seems to me, is what all humans necessarily do; and our feelings and emotions are an integral part of the process.

So, at this point I have left behind the concept of behavioral objectives, the idea that all students should gain the same knowledge and meanings from educational experiences, and the idea that behavioral psychology can provide meaningful insights for human beings. I have come to value the quality of life in the classroom: interest, caring, questioning, sharing, humor, wonder, and love. I know that people create different meaning from the same experience. I cannot generalize about learning as a separate concept but, rather, I observe a person thinking, feeling, and acting in a particular context. I'm not even sure that *learning* is a useful concept.

Whatever curriculum design and guidelines are created for teachers, I believe that the real, live curriculum is how teachers and students together respond to and make meaning from the world around them: what the teacher and each student bring to the classroom to be examined, questioned, acted on, reflected upon, and simply experienced. For every person in the classroom, making the curriculum "is an individual creative process based on their own perception of the world and their own willingness to risk in reaching out as active learners. It is both their being-in-the-world and their becoming."[52]

How have my perceptions changed since 1976, when I wrote those words? I am more aware of sociological interpretations of knowledge and language, and I am more concerned about political pressures. But I still firmly believe that all curriculum workers, and particularly teachers, should try to become aware of their own attitudes and insights, which inescapably are part of their curricular thinking, their decisions about content, and the quality of life in classrooms. Some insights from psychology may be helpful to them; so will insights from other areas such as philosophy and literature.

In Alice Walker's novel, *The Color Purple*, an old man is sitting on a porch in a rural setting, talking to his former wife:

> Anyhow, he say, you know how it is. You ast yourself one question, it lead to fifteen. I started to wonder why us need love. Why us suffer. Why us black. Why us men and women. Where do children really come from. It didn't take long to realize I didn't hardly know nothing. And that if you ast yourself why you black or a man or a woman or a bush it don't mean nothing if you don't ast why you here, period.
>
> So what you think? I ast.
>
> I think us here to wonder, myself. To wonder. To ast. And that in wondering bout the big things and asting bout the big things, you learn about the little ones, almost by accident. But you never know nothing more about the big things than you start with. The more I wonder, he say, the more I love.[53]

Can such insights enter into the thinking of curriculum makers? I believe they can. Schools can be places where we wonder and love, or at least care, as we go about asking questions, thinking, interacting with each other, and attempting to understand our being-in-the-world. We can do this in spite of the fact that the politics of today are hostile to such curricular practices as discussing alternative viewpoints and to such goals as encouraging the wondering and the autonomy of children.

What guides us in our curricular thinking is the world view we have constructed; an integration of our personal histories, our psychological insights, our values, our joint purposes, our social context, and the children with whom we live in the classroom. In order to improve our work we must pause to read, to talk, to reflect on our actions, to expand our awareness, and to reexamine our assumptions. The reader may already be engaged in such continuous reflection. The psychological insights that are embedded in each person's world view should also be challenged in action and dialogue.

It is, I believe, in the sharing of our thinking and the challenging of our beliefs and actions that we expand and reshape our curricular thinking, and our curricular thinking reshapes our actions.

Notes

[1]David Bohm, *Wholeness and the Implicate Order* (London: ARK Paperbacks, 1983), pp. 4-5.

[2]William James, *Talks to Teachers* (New York: Norton, 1958), pp. 23-24.

[3]For a detailed description of different theories, see Morris L. Bigge and Maurice P. Hunt, *Psychological Foundations of Education*, 3rd ed. (New York: Harper and Row, 1980), p. 225 and ch. 19.

[4]For a more technical description of various learning "principles" considered useful to practitioners, see Ernest R. Hilgard and Gordon H. Bower, *Theories of Learning*, 4th ed. (Englewood Cliffs, N.J.: Prentice-Hall, 1975), p. 608.

[5]For a description of this approach, see Robert F. Mager, *Preparing Instructional Objectives*, 2nd ed. (Belmont, Calif.: Fearon-Pitman, 1975); James Popham and Eva Baker, *Establishing Instructional Goals* (Englewood Cliffs, N.J.: Prentice-Hall, 1970).

[6]There are numerous criticisms in the literature. See, for example, Arthur Combs, *Educational Accountability: Beyond Behavioral Objectives* (Alexandria, Va.: Association for Supervision and Curriculum Development, 1972); Noam Chomsky, review of *Beyond Freedom and Dignity*, by B. F. Skinner, in *New York Review of Books* 17 (December 30, 1971), p. 18; James B. Macdonald and Bernice J. Wolfson, "A Case Against Behavioral Objectives," *The Elementary School Journal* 71 (December 1970): 119-128.

[7]Arnold Gesell, *The First Five Years of Life* (New York: Harper, 1940).

[8]Nancy Bayley, *Manual for the Bayley Scales of Infant Development* (New York: The Psychological Corporation, 1969).

[9]Suggested works are: Jerome Bruner and others, *Studies in Cognitive Growth* (New York: Wiley, 1966); Alexander Luria, *Cognitive Development: Its Cultural and Social Foundations* (Cambridge: Harvard University Press, 1976); Jean Piaget, *The Language and Thought of the Child* (London: Routledge and Kegan Paul, 1955); Lev S. Vygotsky, *Thought and Language* (Cambridge: MIT Press and Wiley, 1962).

[10]Kenneth Goodman, *Language and Literacy*, Vols. 1 and 2 (Boston: Routledge and Kegan Paul, 1982); Frank Smith, *Psycholinguistics and Reading* (New York: Holt, Rinehart and Winston, 1973).

[11]Erik H. Erikson, *Childhood and Society*, rev. ed. (New York: Norton, 1963); Sigmund Freud, *New Introductory Lectures on Psychoanalysis*, ed. and trans. James Strachey (New York: Norton, 1965).

[12]Piaget recognized that cultural contexts would affect rates of development; however, Vygotsky and Luria saw the cultural and the biological interlacing at each stage of the child's development. "While Piaget stresses biologically supported universal stages of development, Vygotsky's emphasis is on the interaction between social

conditions and the biological substrata of behavior." Vera John-Steiner and Ellen Souberman in Vygotsky, *Mind in Society*, eds. Michael Cole and others (Cambridge: Harvard University Press, 1978), p. 123.

[13]Piaget believed that "the principal goal of education is to create men who are capable of doing new things, not simply of repeating what other generations have done—men who are creative, inventive, and discoverers. The second goal of education is to form minds which can be critical, can verify, and not accept everything they are offered." From Eleanor Duckworth, in *Piaget Rediscovered* (a report of the Conference on Cognition Studies and Curriculum Development), eds. Richard E. Ripple and Vern N. Rockcastle (Ithaca: Cornell University School of Education, 1964), p. 5.

[14]See Arthur Combs and others, *Perceptual Psychology: A Humanistic Approach to the Study of Persons* (New York: Harper and Row, 1976), chapters 8 and 9; Rollo May, ed., *Existential Psychology* (New York: Random House, 1961), chapters 1, 2, and 5; Abraham Maslow, *Motivation and Personality*, 2nd ed. (New York: Harper, 1954); Carl Rogers, *On Becoming A Person* (Boston: Houghton Mifflin, 1961).

[15]See Maxine Greene, *Landscapes of Learning* (New York: Teachers College Press, 1978); Carl Rogers, *Freedom to Learn for the 80's*, rev. (Columbus, Ohio: C. E. Merrill Publishing Co., 1983).

[16]Both Combs and Rogers refer to research testing their theories.

[17]Constance Kamii and Rheta DeVries, "Piaget for Early Education," in *The Preschool in Action*, 2nd ed., eds. M. C. Day and R. K. Parker (Boston: Allyn and Bacon, 1977).

[18]Described in Jerome Bruner, *Toward A Theory of Instruction* (Cambridge: Harvard University Press, 1966), pp. 73-101.

[19]See Arthur Combs, *A Personal Approach to Teaching: Beliefs That Make a Difference* (Boston: Allyn and Bacon, 1982); Carl Rogers, *Freedom to Learn*.

[20]Jerome Bruner, *In Search of Mind: Essays in Autobiography* (New York: Harper and Row, 1983), p. 8.

[21]Ibid., p. 184.

[22]Ibid., p. 278.

[23]Ibid., p. 185.

[24]Jerome Bruner, *The Relevance of Education* (New York: W. W. Norton, 1973), p. 56.

[25]Ibid., p. 57.

[26]Ibid., p. 57.

[27]Ibid., p. 58.

[28]Bruner, 1983, p. 198. For accounts of the controversies, see *Educational Leadership* (November 1976): 105-117.

[29]Jerome Bruner and others, *Studies in Cognitive Growth* (New York: John Wiley and Sons, 1966), chapters 1 and 2.

[30]Carl Rogers, *Freedom to Learn*, p. 2.

[31]Ibid., p. 3.

[32]Ibid., p. 20.

[33]Ibid., p. 18.

[34]Ibid., pp. 135-136.

[35]Ibid., p. 136.

[36]Ibid., pp. 227-250.

[37]Willard Jacobson and Allan Kondo, *SCIS Elementary Science Sourcebook*, Trial ed. (Berkeley, Calif.: Science Improvement Study, University of California, 1968), pp. 26-39; Robert Karplus and others, *Interactions and Systems*, Level 2, Teachers Guide, Science Improvement Study (New York: Rand McNally, 1978).

[38]Margaret M. Clark, *Young Fluent Readers* (London: Heinemann Educational Books, 1976); Marie Clay, *Observing Young Readers* (London: Heinemann Educational Books, 1982).

[39]Kenneth Goodman, "Reading: A Psycholinguistic Guessing Game," *The Journal of the Reading Specialist* 6, 4: 126-135.

[40]Frank Smith, *Understanding Reading* (New York: Holt, Rinehart and Winston, 1971), p. 181.

[41]Smith, p. 186.

[42]Luria, *Cognitive Development*, p. 163.

[43]See John Naisbitt, *Megatrends* (New York: Warner Books, 1982); Alvin Toffler, *Previews and Premises* (New York: William Morrow, 1983).

[44]See Sherry Turkle, *The Second Self: Computers and the Human Spirit* (New York: Simon and Schuster, 1984).

[45]Decker Walker, "Reflections on the Educational Potential and Limitations of Microcomputers," *Phi Delta Kappan* 65, 2: 103-107.

[46]See Carol Gilligan, *In a Different Voice* (Cambridge: Harvard University Press, 1982); Judith Jean Baker Miller, *Toward A New Psychology of Women* (Boston: Beacon Press, 1976).

[47]See Nancy Frazier and Myra Sadker, *Sexism in School and Society* (New York: Harper and Row, 1973); Dale Spender, *Invisible Women* (London: Writers and Readers, 1982); Barbara Sprung, ed., *Perspectives on Non-sexist Early Childhood Education* (New York: Teachers Press, 1978).

[48]See Barbara B. Brown, *Supermind: The Ultimate Energy* (New York: Bantam Books, 1983).

[49]See Jerre Levy, "Research Synthesis on Right and Left Hemispheres: We Think with Both Sides of the Brain," *Educational Leadership* (January 1983): 66-71.

[50]Michael Polanyi, *The Study of Man* (Chicago: The University of Chicago Press, 1958), p. 22.

[51]Combs and Snygg, *Individual Psychology*. See Arthur Combs, *Perceptual Psychology: A Humanistic Approach to the Study of Persons* (New York: Harper and Row, 1976), and *Educational Accountability: Beyond Behavioral Objectives.*

[52]Bernice J. Wolfson, "A Phenomenological Perspective on Curriculum and Learning," in Alex Molnar and John Zahorik, eds., *Curriculum Theory* (Alexandria, Va., Association for Supervision and Curriculum Development, 1977), p. 87.

[53]Alice Walker, *The Color Purple* (New York: Harcourt Brace, 1982), p. 247.

Chapter 5.
Making Knowledge Legitimate: Power, Profit, and The Textbook

MICHAEL W. APPLE

*W*hose culture is it that gets into schools? Yours? Mine? The culture of elite and powerful groups? Or is it more complicated than that? What powers determine what gets taught in the classroom or lecture hall? Who makes such important decisions? These are difficult questions, to say the least. In order to make some headway in answering them it will be necessary to look first not inside the school, where most of us are more comfortable, but somewhere else. We need to consider how culture is thought about politically and economically.

It is possible to consider culture in two ways: (1) as a lived process, as what could be called a whole way of life, or (2) as a commodity.[1] If culture is considered as a lived process, we focus on it as the major social process through which we live our daily lives. If we consider culture a commodity, we emphasize the *products* of culture, the commodities we produce and consume. This distinction can, of course, be maintained only on an analytic level, since most of the products of our culture, things like lightbulbs, cars, records, and, in the case of this essay, books, are really part of a larger social

Michael W. Apple is Professor of Curriculum and Instruction and Educational Policy Studies, University of Wisconsin-Madison.

Author's note: *I would like to thank Rima D. Apple, Neal Earls, Ruth Earls, Linda McNeil, Alex Molnar, Peter Musgrave, Steven Selden, and the members of the seminar on Ideology and Curriculum at the University of Wisconsin for their comments on various versions of this chapter.*

process. As a number of social theorists spent years trying to demonstrate, every product is an expression of embodied human labor. Goods and services are, in fact, relations among people—relations of unequal resources and power often but human relations nevertheless. Turning on a light when you walk into a room is not only using an object but also being involved in an anonymous social relationship with the miner who worked to dig the coal burned to produce the electricity.

This dual process-product nature of culture poses a dilemma for educators who are interested in understanding the dynamics of popular and elite culture in our society. It complicates studying the dominant cultural products inside and outside of the school—films, books, television programs, music—for there are sets of relations behind each of these "things." And these relations are, in turn, situated within the larger web of the social and market relations of our economy.

Although it is necessary to avoid the trap of oversimplifying and seeing everything as determined solely by money and power, it is essential that we look more closely at this political economy of culture in order to understand how things come to be taught in school. How do the dynamics of class, gender, and race "determine" cultural production? How is the organization and distribution of culture "mediated" by economic and social structures?[2] What is the relationship between a cultural product, such as a film or a schoolbook, and the social relations of its production, distribution, and consumption?[3]

Even though the overt aim of schools is cultural transmission, it only has been in the last decade or so that the politics and economics of the culture that actually *is* transmitted in schools has been taken up as a serious research problem. It is almost as if Durkheim and Weber, to say nothing of Marx, had never existed. In the area currently called the sociology of the curriculum, however, a good deal of progress has been made in understanding *whose* knowledge is taught in and produced for our schools[4]

While not the only questions with which we should be concerned, it is clear that content and organization are major curriculum issues. What should be taught? In what way? Answering these is difficult. The first question not only involves some very hard epistemological questions—for example, what should be granted the status of knowledge?—but it is politically loaded as well. To borrow the language of Pierre Bourdieu and Basil Bernstein, the "cultural capital" of dominant classes and groups has been considered the most legitimate knowledge.[5] Further, this knowledge, and one's "ability" to deal with it, is one of the mechanisms in a complex process in which the unequal class, gender, and race relations of our society are reproduced. Therefore, the choice of particular content and ways of approaching it in schools is related both to existing power relations and to conflicts over altering these relations as well. Not to recognize this is to ignore a wealth of evidence in the United States, England, Australia, France, Sweden, Germany, and elsewhere that links school knowledge—both commodified and lived—to class, gender, and race relationships outside as well as inside schools.[6]

Simply recognizing the political nature of the curriculum does not solve all of our problems, however. The statement that school knowledge is connected to our political economy merely restates the issue. It does not in itself explain how such connections operate. Though the ties that link curriculums to the inequities and conflicts in our society are complicated, there is research that helps illuminate these connections. The most interesting, focusing on the culture and commerce of publishing, examines how publishing operates internally, its social relations and composition, and its cultural and economic context. What do the social and economic relations within the publishing industry have to do with schools, with the politics of knowledge distribution in education? Perhaps this can be made clearer if we first consider the following question.

How is "legitimate" knowledge made available in schools? By and large it is through something we have paid far too little attention to—the textbook. Whether we like it or not, the curriculum in most American schools is not defined by courses of study or suggested programs, but by one particular artifact, the standardized, grade-level-specific text in mathematics, reading, social studies, science, and so on.

The impact of textbooks on the social relations of the classroom is also immense. It is estimated, for example, that 75 percent of the time that elementary and secondary students are in classrooms and 90 percent of their time on homework is spent with text materials.[7] Yet, even given the ubiquitous character of the textbook, it is one of the things we know about least. While the text dominates curriculums at the elementary, secondary, and even college levels, little critical attention has been paid to the ideological, political, and economic sources of its production, distribution, and reception.[8]

The production of curricular materials such as texts is part of the larger process of the production of cultural commodities, such as books, in general. Yet of the approximately 40,000 books published each year in the United States, only a small portion are textbooks.[9] Despite the variety of books published, certain constants affect publishers.

We can identify four major structural conditions that shape publishing in the United States.

(1) The industry sells its products—like any commodity—in a market, but a market that, in contrast to that for many other products, is fickle and often uncertain. (2) The industry is decentralized among a number of sectors whose operations bear little resemblance to each other. (3) These operations are characterized by a mixture of modern mass-production methods and craft-like procedures. (4) The industry remains perilously poised between the require-ments and restraints of commerce and the responsibilities and obligations that it must bear as a prime guardian of the symbolic culture of the nation. Although the tensions between the claims of commerce and culture seem to us always to have been with book publishing, they have become more acute and salient in the last twenty years.[10]

These conditions are not new phenomena by any means. From the time printing began as an industry, books were pieces of merchandise. They were, of course, often produced for scholarly or humanistic purposes, but before anything else their prime function was to earn their producers a living. Book production, hence, has historically rested on a foundation where from the outset it was necessary to "find enough capital to start work and then to print only those titles which would satisfy a clientele, and at a price which would withstand competition."[11] As in the marketing of other products, then, finance and costing took an immensely important place in the decisions of publishers and booksellers.[12]

The idea of capital, if used cautiously, can help us to go a bit further here. Drawing upon Pierre Bourdieu's work, we can make a distinction between two types of "capital," *symbolic* and *financial*. This enables us to distinguish among the many kinds of publishers to gauge what their strategies will be in dealing with knowledge. In essence, these two kinds of capital are found in different kinds of markets. Those firms that are more commercial, that are oriented to rapid turnover, quick obsolescence, and to the minimization of risks are following a strategy for the accumulation of financial capital. Such a strategy has a short time perspective, one that focuses on the current interests of a particular group of readers. In contradistinction to those firms, companies whose goal is the accumulation of symbolic capital have a longer time per-spective. Immediate profit is less important. Higher risks may be taken, and experimental content and form find greater acceptance. These publishers are not uninterested in the "logic of profitability," but long-term profit is more important. One example is provided by Beckett's *Waiting for Godot*, which sold only 10,000 copies in the first five years after its publication in 1952, yet then went on to sell 60,000 copies as its rate of sales increased yearly by 20 percent.[13]

This conceptual distinction based on varying kinds of capital does not totally cover the differences in the kinds of books publishers publish, however.

Coser, Kadushin, and Powell, for example, further classify publishers according to the ways in which editors themselves carry out their work. In so doing, they distinguish among trade publishers, text publishers, and the various scholarly monograph or university presses. Each of these labels refers to more than just editorial policy. Together, they speak to a whole array of differences concerning the kind of technology that is employed by the press, the bureaucratic and organizational structures that coordinate and control the day-to-day work of the company, and the risks and monetary and marketing policies of each. Each also refers to important differences in relations with authors, in time scheduling, and ultimately in what counts as "success."[14] Thus it should be clear that behind the commodity—the book—indeed stands a whole set of human relations. By integrating the analyses of internal decision-making processes and external market relations within publishing, we should gain insight into how particular aspects of popular and elite culture are presented in published form for sale to schools throughout the United States and elsewhere.

Let us set the stage historically for our further discussion. From the period just after the Civil War to the first decade of the 20th century, fiction led in the sheer quantity of titles that were published. We can see this if we take one year as an example. In 1886 *Publishers Weekly* took the nearly 5,000 books published that year and divided them into various categories. The ten with the most volumes were: fiction (1,080), law (469), juvenile (458), literary history and miscellaneous (388), theology (377), education and language (275), poetry and drama (220), history (182), medical science (177), and social and political science (174).[15] These data do not account for the many informal political booklets and pamphlets that were published.

The composition of the readership, literacy rates, and the economic conditions of publishing and purchasing all had an impact on what was published. But it is not simply that certain types of books are published but *why* they are published that is of great importance. To understand this it is necessary to take social factors into account. Market constraints, for example, have often had a profound impact on what gets published and even on what authors write. Certain aspects of fiction writing and publishing offer an interesting case in point. Wendy Griswold's analysis of the manner in which different market positions occupied by various authors and publishers had an impact documents this nicely.

In the 19th century, the topics favored by European writers had a distinct market advantage in the United States due to the oddities of our copyright laws. As Griswold puts it:

During most of the 19th century, American copyright laws protected citizens or permanent residents of the United States but not foreign authors. The result was that British and other foreign works could be reprinted and sold in the United States without royalties being paid to their authors, while Americans did receive royalty payments. Many interests in the United States benefited from this literary piracy and lobbied to maintain the status quo. (Actually piracy is something of a misnomer, for the practice was perfectly legal.) The nascent printing industry was kept busy. Publishers made huge profits from reprinting foreign books. Readers had available the best foreign literature at low prices; for example, in 1843 *A Christmas Carol* sold for 6¢ in the United States and the equivalent of $2.50 in England.[16]

Clearly, such a situation created problems for authors. American publishers had little inducement to publish "original native works," since a copyright had to be paid to their authors. American authors were largely left, then, unable to earn their living as fiction writers because they were excluded from the market. This also had an impact on the very content of their writing. Since they were discouraged from dealing with subjects already treated in the cheaper editions of European works, American authors often had to stake out a different terrain, areas that were unusual but would still have enough market appeal to convince publishers to publish them.[17]

These influences did not constitute a new phenomenon. In fact, the growth of particular genres and the styles of books themselves have been linked closely to similar social forces operating earlier. As Ian Watt and Raymond Williams have argued, the rise of the novel was related to, among other things, changes in the political economy and class structure and to the growth of an ideology of individualism in Europe and the United States.[18] In the 18th century, for instance, "the rapid expansion of a new audience for literature, the literate middle class, especially the leisured middle class women," led to novels focusing on "love and marriage, economic individualism, the complexities of modern life, and the possibility of personal morality in a corrupting world." The economic conditions of publishing changed as well. There was a decline in private support for authors and the growth of the bookseller who published, printed, and sold books. Authors were often paid by the page, so speed and length of the work became important.[19]

Book publishing today lives in the shadow of these historical influences. Thus, this background is particularly helpful in understanding the commercial and cultural structures involved in the publication of textbooks today. An excellent case in point is the production of texts for, say, college-level courses. The "culture and commerce" of college-text production provides some important insights into how the cultural commodification process works, insights that will help us understand the nature of textbooks at all levels in our educational system.

The Business of Publishing

While we may think of book publishing as a relatively large industry, by current standards it is actually rather small when compared to others. The *entire* book publishing industry with its 65,000 or so employees would rank nearly 40 to 50 positions below a single one of the highest grossing and largest employing American companies. While the industry's total sales in 1980 were approximately $6 billion, in many ways its market is much less certain and is subject to greater economic, political, and ideological contingencies than many larger companies.

Six billion dollars, though, is still definitely not a pittance. Book publishing *is* an industry, one that is divided up into a variety of markets. Of the $6-billion total, $1.2 billion was accounted for by reference books, encyclopedias, and professional books; $1.5 billion came from the elementary, secondary, and college text market; $1 billion was taken in from book clubs and direct mail sales; nearly $660 million came from mass market paperbacks; and, finally, books intended for the general public (trade books) brought $1 billion. With its $1.5 billion sales, the textbook market is obviously one of the largest segments of the industry.[20]

There has been a marked increase in concentration of power in the text publishing industry. While competition has increased recently, it has been among a smaller number of firms. The nature of this competition has reduced the willingness of firms to take risks. Instead, many text publishers now prefer to expend most of their efforts on a smaller selection of "carefully chosen 'products.'"[21]

Perhaps the simplest way to illuminate this competitive dynamic is to quote a major figure in publishing who, after 35 years in the industry, reflected on the question, "How competitive is book publishing?" His one-word answer— "Very."[22]

A picture of the concentration within text publishing can be complied from a few facts. The 10 largest text publishers sell 75 percent of all college textbooks; the top 20 publishers account for 90 percent of all sales. Prentice-Hall; McGraw-Hill; the CBS Publishing Group; and Scott, Foresman—the top four—account for 40 percent of the market.[23] In what is called the "elhi" (elementary and high school) market, the figures are equally revealing. It is estimated that the four largest textbook publishers in this field account for 32 percent of the market. The eight largest firms control 53 percent. And the 20 largest control more than 75 percent of sales.[24] Yet concentration does not tell the entire story. Internal qualities are also important, such as who works in these firms, their backgrounds, their characteristics, and their working conditions.

What kind of people make the decisions about college and other texts? Many people find their way into publishing by accident, including textbook editors. "Most of them entered publishing simply because they were looking for some sort of job, and publishing presented itself."[25] But these people are not all equal. Important divisions of power exist within the publishing houses themselves.

Recent research, for example, reveals the pervasiveness of sex-typing in the division of labor in publishing. Women are often found in subsidiary rights and publicity departments. They are often copy editors. While they outnumber men in employment within publishing as a whole, this does not mean that they exert a powerful overt force. Rather, they tend to largely be hired as "secretaries, assistants, publicists, advertising managers, and occupants of other low- and mid-level positions." Even though a number of women have moved into important editorial positions in the past few years, by and large they are still not as evident as men in positions that actually "exercise control over the goals and policy of publishing." In essence, there is something of a dual labor market in publishing. The lower paying, replaceable jobs, with less possibility for advancement, are characteristically "female enclaves."[26]

What does this mean for our discussion? Nearly 75 percent of the editors in college-text publishing either began their careers in sales or held sales or marketing positions before being promoted to editor.[27] Since there are many fewer women than men who sell college or other texts or hold positions of authority within sales departments that could lead to upward mobility, this has an effect both on the people who become editors and consequently on the content of editorial decisions.

These facts have important implications. Most editorial decisions concerning which texts are to be published—and ultimately what reaches students as "official knowledge" within particular disciplines— are made by individuals who have specific characteristics. These editors will be predominantly male, thereby reproducing patriarchal relations within the firm itself. Second, their general background will complement the existing market structure that dominates text production. Financial capital, short-term perspectives, and high profit margins will be seen as major goals.[28] A substantial cultural or educational vision or the concerns associated with strategies based on symbolic capital will necessarily take a back seat, where they exist at all.

The influence of profit, of the power of what they call "commerce" in text production, is recognized by Coser, Kadushin, and Powell. They note that in college text publishing, the major emphasis is on the production of books for introductory level courses that have high student enrollments. A good deal of attention is paid to the design of the book itself and to marketing strategies that will lead to its use in these courses.[29] Yet unlike most other kinds of publishing, text publishers define their market not as the actual reader of the book but as the teacher or professor.[30] The purchaser, the student, has little power in this equation, except where it may influence a professor's decision.

Based on the sense of sales potential and on their "regular polling of their market," a large percentage of college text editors actively search for books. Contacts are made, suggestions given. In essence, it would not be wrong to say that text editors create their own books.[31]

In the United States it is estimated that the production cost of an introductory text for a college level course is usually between $100,000 and $250,000. Given the fact that text publishers produce a relatively few number of books compared to publishers of, say, fiction, there is considerable pressure on the editorial staff and others to guarantee that such books sell.[32] For the "elhi" market the sheer amount of money and the risks involved are apparent in the fact that for every $500,000 invested by a publisher in a text, 100,000 copies needed to be sold merely to break even.[33]

These conditions have ramifications for the social relations within the firm in addition to the male-dominated structure. Staff meetings, meetings with other editors, meetings with marketing and production staff to coordinate the production of a text, and other such activities dominate the life of the text editor. As Coser and his co-authors so nicely phrase it, "text editors practially live in meetings."[34] Hence, text publishing will be quite bureaucratic and will have a very formalized decision-making structure. This is partly due to the fact that textbook production is largely a routine process. Formats do not differ markedly from discipline to discipline. The focus is primarily on producing a limited number of big sellers at a comparatively high price (as compared, for example, to fiction). Last, the emphasis is often on marketing a standard text that, with revisions and a little luck, will be used for years to come.[35]

Such elements of bureaucratization and standardization are heightened even more in the production of "managed" texts. These are texts written, for the most part, by professional writers with some "guidance" from graduate students and academics, and often bearing the name of a well-known professor. In many ways, they are books without formal authors. Ghost written under stringent cost controls, geared to what will sell—not necessarily what is most important to know—managed texts are taking their place in many college classrooms. While some publishers dream that managed texts will solve their financial problems, such hopes have not been totally realized. Still, the managed text is a significant phenomenon that deserves a good deal of critical attention, not only at the college level but also in elementary and secondary schools, since managed texts can be found there too.

Although some managed texts have not reaped anticipated profits, the trend toward more centralized control over the entire process of publishing material for classroom use is likely to continue. The effect, according to Coser, Kadushin, and Powell, will be "an even greater homogenization of texts at a college level,"[37] something we can expect at the elementary and high school level as well.[38]

Censorship by Profitability

One would expect that all of the meetings, the planning, the growing sampling of markets, the competition, and so forth would have a profound impact on the content of volumes. This is the case, but not quite in the way one might think. Even though existing research does not go into detail about how, specifically, book content is determined within the college text industry, one can infer the process from what research says about censorship in the publishing industry as a whole.

In the increasingly conglomerate-dominated publishing industry, censorship and ideological control, as we commonly think of them, are less of a problem than might be anticipated. It is not ideological uniformity or some political agenda that accounts for many of the ideas that are ultimately made or not made available to the larger public. Rather, it is the infamous "bottom line" that counts. "Ultimately ... if there is any censorship, it concerns profitability. Books that are not profitable, no matter what their subject, are not viewed favorably."[39]

This is not a minor concern. In the publishing industry as a whole, only three out of every ten books are marginally profitable. Another 30 percent break even. The remainder lose money.[40] Further, it has become clear that sales of texts have been declining. If we take as a baseline the years of 1968 to 1976, costs rose considerably while sales at the college level fell 10 percent. Though the situation is changing somewhat today, the same was true for the "elhi" text market: Coupled with rising costs, sales dropped 11.2 percent.[41] Thus profit questions limit what are considered to be rational choices in corporate publishing.

Does the fact that profitability generally shapes content in the publishing industry mean that profit also plays a large role in determining the content of standardized secondary and elementary textbooks? Are market, profit, and internal relations more important than ideological concerns in determining schoolbook content? This is only partially the case.

The economics and politics of text production appear somewhat more complicated when one examines what is produced for sale to our elementary and secondary schools. While there is no official federal government sponsorship of specific curriculum content in the United States, compared with countries where ministries of education mandate a standard course of study, a structured national curriculum is nonetheless produced in other ways by the marketplace and by state intervention. Perhaps the most important aspect of this situation revolves around the various models now extant for the statewide adoption of textbooks.

In many states—mainly from the southern tier around to the western Sun Belt—textbooks in major subject areas must be approved by state agencies or committees. Or they are reviewed, and a limited number are recommended for use in schools. Local school districts that select from such approved lists are often reimbursed for a significant portion of the purchase cost. Even where texts are not mandated, local schools have a good deal to gain in times of economic crisis if they choose an approved volume. The savings can be substantial.

Yet it is not only here that the economics of cultural distribution operates. Publishers themselves, simply because of good business practice, must aim their product toward those states with text review policies. Simply getting one's volume on such a list can ensure a text's profitability. For example, sales to California and Texas (both of which adopt texts statewide) can account for more than 20 percent of a book's total sales, a considerable percentage in the highly competitive world of schoolbook publishing. Hence, writing, editing, and promotion of such texts are quite often aimed at earning a place on the list of state-approved material.

The political and ideological climate of these primarily southern states often determines the content and form of curriculums purchased throughout the nation. And since a textbook series often takes years to write and produce, "publishers want assurance of knowing that their school book series will sell before they commit large budgets to these undertakings."[42]

The situation is complicated by the fact that serious conflicts often arise in these states and their curriculum agencies over whose knowledge should be taught. These very conflicts may make it very difficult for publishers to determine what the needs of "financial capital" actually are and what content has the best chance of being approved. Given the uncertainty of a market, publishers may be loath to make decisions based on the "needs" of any one state, especially in highly charged curriculum areas. A good example is provided in California by the creationism vs. evolutionism controversy, where a group of "scientific creationists" supported by the political and ideological right sought to have all social studies and science texts give equal weight to creationist and evolutionary theories. Even when the state Board of Education recommended "editorial qualifications" to meet the objections of creationists, the framework for text adoption remained unclear and subject to many interpretations. For example, did the new guidelines require or merely allow discussion of creation theory? Were editorial changes that slightly qualified the discussions of evolution all that was required?

Given this ambiguity and the volatility of the issue in which the "winning position" was unclear, publishers "resisted undertaking the more substantial effort of incorporating new information into their materials."[43] As one observer noted, "Faced with an unclear directive, and one that might be reversed at any moment, publishers were reluctant to invest in change. They eventually yielded to the minor editorial adjustments adopted by the board, but staunchly resisted the requirement that they discuss creation in their social science texts."[44] Both economic and ideological forces are highly evident between the firms and their markets and undoubtedly within each firm.

Notice what this means if we are to fully understand how specific cultural goods are produced and distributed for our public schools. What at first glance seems relatively simple gets more complicated once we dig beneath the surface. Once again we find ourselves grappling with a fairly complicated set of interrelationships. How does the political economy of publishing itself generate particular ideological needs? How and why do publishers respond to the needs of the "public"? Who determines what this "public" is?[45] How do the internal politics of state-adoption policies work? What are the processes by which people are selected to sit on such committees? How are texts marketed at a local level? What is the actual process of text production, from the commissioning of a project to revisions and editing to promotion and sales? Only by going into considerable detail on such questions can we begin to see how a particular group's "cultural capital" is turned into a commodity and made available (or not made available) in schools throughout the country.[46]

My discussion is not meant to imply that all of the material found in our public schools will simply reflect existing cultural and economic inequalities. After all, if texts were totally reliable defenders of the existing ideological, political, and economic order, they would not be such a contentious area today. Industry and conservative groups have made an issue of what knowledge is now taught in schools precisely because there *are* progressive elements within curriculums and texts.[47] This is partly due to the fact that the authorship and editing of such material is often done by a particular segment of the middle class with its own, largely liberal, ideological values and its own sense of what is important to know. These values will not necessarily be identical to those embodied in profit maximization or ideological uniformity, and they may be a bit more progressive than one might anticipate given the market structure of text production. Surely, they militate against total standardization and censorship in the production of school texts.[48]

Conclusion

Some of my arguments in this chapter have been abstract, but they are important to our progress in building models of curriculum theory and research that take seriously the dominance of commercially produced materials in schools and colleges. For those of us who want to understand why texts look the way they do (as I think we all should want to), certain tendencies are now clearer. Caught within a changing set of market relations which set limits on what is considered rational behavior on the part of its participants, editors and other employees have some autonomy. They are partly free to pursue the internal needs of their craft and to follow the logic of internal demands within the publishing house itself. The past histories of gender, class, and ethnic relations and the actual "local" political economy of publishing set the boundaries within which these decisions are made and in large part determine who will make the decisions.

To return to my earlier point about text editors usually having their roots in sales, we can see that the internal labor market in text publishing, the ladder upon which career mobility depends, means that sales will be in the forefront ideologically and economically in these firms. "Finance capital" dominates, not only because the economy "out there" mandates it, but because of other things as well. Among the factors with an impact are the historical development of mobility patterns within firms, rational decision making based on external competition, political dynamics, and internal information. This kind of analysis is complicated but manages to preserve the power of the economy while granting some autonomy to the internal bureaucratic and biographical structure of individual publishers. At the same time, it recognizes the political economy of gendered labor that exists as well.

There are many areas that I have not focused on in this chapter. Among the most important is the alteration in the technology of publishing. We should expect that the massive ongoing changes in the technology of text production will also have a serious impact on future books. At the very least, given the sexual division of labor in publishing, new technologies can have a large bearing on the de-skilling and re-skilling of "female enclaves" and on the power of women as decision makers within these firms.[49]

Further, even though I have directed my attention primarily to the "culture and commerce" surrounding the production of one particular cultural commodity, standardized texts used for tertiary and other level courses, I have only scratched the surface of the politics that stands behind their selection. A good deal remains to be done on how exactly the economic and ideological elements I have outlined actually work through one of the largest of all text markets—elementary and secondary schools in the United States and elsewhere. For it is here that what counts as legitimate knowledge is largely determined.

This points to the need for empirical research as well. What is required now is a long-term *and* theoretically and politically grounded ethnographic investigation that follows a curriculum artifact, such as a textbook, from its writing to its selling (and then to its use). Not only would this be a major contribution to our understanding of the relationship among culture, politics, and economy in education, it would also be absolutely essential if we are to act in ways that alter the kinds of knowledge considered legitimate for transmission in our schools.[50] As long as the text dominates curriculums, ignoring it as not worthy of serious attention is to live in a world divorced from reality.

In this chapter I have gone behind the scenes to examine some of the historical and current reasons textbooks look the way they do. And I have provided an example of a particular kind of curriculum thinking, one that places some of the major curriculum problems we face as teachers, administrators, and curriculum workers within their larger social and economic context. I have argued that it is important to recognize this context if we truly want to get better and more representative knowledge in our schools. In a time when schools and their curriculums are clearly becoming political and economic footballs, it is exactly this kind of curriculum thinking that is most necessary.

The current hue and cry over the weaknesses of textbooks will wax and wane, but none of us will have more than a token impact unless we more fully understand the *business* of publishing. As long as the tail of a few states wags the dog of the rest of the country, the economics of adoption policies may largely preclude better texts. As long as profit is the first consideration, we may be faced with a situation in which the content we teach is not determined by *democratic* deliberation but by the "invisible" hand of the market. The most significant question we can ask now is, "Are there better and more democratic ways to determine how texts are published?" Answers will not be easy to come by, but whoever said that trying to provide the best education possible for our children was going to be easy?

Notes

My arguments in this chapter are based on a longer analysis forthcoming in the *Journal of Curriculum Studies*.

[1]See Michael W. Apple and Lois Weis, eds., *Ideology and Practice in Schooling* (Philadelphia: Temple University Press, 1983), especially chapter 1.

[2]Janet Wolff, *The Social Production of Art* (London: Macmillan, 1981), p. 47.

[3]These issues are dealt with in greater detail in Michael W. Apple, ed., *Cultural and Economic Reproduction in Education: Essays on Class, Ideology and the State* (Boston: Routledge and Kegan Paul, 1982).

[4]Michael W. Apple, *Ideology and Curriculum* (Boston: Routledge and Kegan Paul, 1979). It is important to realize, however, that educational institutions are *not* merely engaged in transmission or distribution. For further discussion of what else our educational institutions do, see Michael W. Apple, *Education and Power* (Boston: Routledge and Kegan Paul, 1982), especially chapter 2.

[5]Pierre Bourdieu and Jean-Claude Passeron, *Reproduction in Education, Society and Culture* (Beverly Hills: Sage, 1977); and Basil Bernstein, *Class, Codes and Control*, Vol. 3 (Boston: Routledge and Kegan Paul, 1977).

[6]For an analysis of recent theoretical and empirical work on the connections between education and cultural, economic, and political power, see Apple, *Education and Power*.

[7]Paul Goldstein, *Changing the American Schoolbook* (Lexington, Mass.: D. C. Heath, 1978), p. 1. On which subjects are taught the most, see John I. Goodlad, *A Place Called School* (New York: McGraw-Hill, 1983).

[8]I do not want to ignore the importance of the massive number of textbook analyses that concern themselves with, say, racism and sexism. These are significant, but are usually limited to the question of balance in content, not the relationship between economic and cultural power. Some of the best analyses of the content and form of educational materials can be found in Apple and Weis, eds., *Ideology and Practice in Schooling*. See also, Sherry Keith, "Politics of Textbook Selection," Institute for Research on Educational Finance and Governance, Stanford University, April 1981.

[9]Lewis Coser, Charles Kadushin, and Walter Powell, *Books: The Culture and Commerce of Publishing* (New York: Basic Books, 1982), p. 3.

[10]Ibid., p. 7.

[11]Lucien Febvre and Henri-Jean Martin, *The Coming of the Book* (London: New Left Books, 1976), p. 109. As Febvre and Martin make clear, however, in the 15th and 16th centuries printers and publishers did act as well as "the protectors of literary men," publish daring books, and frequently sheltered authors accused of heresy. See p. 150.

[12]Ibid.

[13]Ibid., p. 44.

[14]Ibid., p. 54.

[15]Wendy Griswold, "American Character and the American Novel: An Expansion of Reflection Theory in the Sociology of Literature," *American Journal of Sociology* 86 (January 1981): 742.

[16]Ibid., p. 748.

[17]Ibid., pp. 748-749.

[18]See Ian Watt, *The Rise of the Novel* (Berkeley: University of California Press, 1974) and Raymond Williams, *The Long Revolution* (London: Chatto and Windus, 1961).

[19]Griswold, "American Character and the American Novel," p. 743.

[20]Leonard Shatzkin, *In Cold Type* (Boston: Houghton and Mifflin, 1982), pp. 1-2. For estimated figures for years beyond 1980, see John P. Dessauer, *Book Industry Trends, 1982* (New York: Book Industry Study Group, Inc., 1982).

[21]Coser, Kadushin, and Powell, *Books*, p. 273. While I focus on text production here, we should not assume that texts are the only books used in elementary, secondary, and college markets. The expanding market of other material can have a strong influence in publishing decisions. In fact, some mass-market paperbacks are clearly prepared with both school and college sales in the forefront of their decisions. Thus, it is not unusual for publishers to produce a volume with very different covers depending on the audience for which it is aimed. See Benjamin M. Compaine, *The Book Industry in Transition: An Economic Study of Book Distribution and Marketing* (White Plains, N.Y.: Knowledge Industry Publications, 1978), p. 95.

[22]Shatzkin, *In Cold Type*, p. 63.

[23]Coser, Kadushin, and Powell, *Books*, p. 273.

[24]Goldstein, *Changing The American Schoolbook*, p. 61.

[25]Coser, Kadushin, and Powell, *Books*, p. 100.

[26]Ibid., pp. 154-155.

[27]Ibid., p. 101.

[28]Coser, Kadushin, and Powell, however, do report that most editors, no matter what kind of house they work for, tend to be overwhelmingly liberal. Ibid., p. 113.

[29]Ibid., p. 30.

[30]Ibid., p. 56.

[31]Ibid., p. 135.

[32]Ibid., pp. 56-57.

[33]Goldstein, *Changing The American Schoolbook*, p. 56.

[34]Coser, Kadushin, and Powell, *Books*, p. 123.

[35]Ibid., p. 190.

[36]Keith, "Politics of Textbook Selection," p. 12.

[37]Coser, Kadushin, and Powell, *Books*, p. 366.

[38]I have discussed this at greater length in Michael W. Apple, "Curriculum in the Year 2,000: Tensions and Possibilities," *Phi Delta Kappan* 64 (January 1983): 321-326.

[39]Ibid., p. 181.

[40]Compaine, *The Book Industry in Transition*, p. 20.

[41]Ibid., pp. 33-34.

[42]Keith, "Politics of Textbook Selection," p. 8.

[43]Goldstein, *Changing the American Schoolbook*, p. 47.

[44]Ibid., pp. 48-49.

[45]For an interesting discussion of how economic needs help determine what counts as the public for which a specific cultural product is aimed, see the treatment

of changes in the radio sponsorship of country music in Richard A. Peterson, "The Production of Cultural Change: The Case of Contemporary Country Music," *Social Research* 45 (Summer 1978): 292-314. See also Paul DiMaggio and Michael Useem, "The Arts in Class Reproduction," in Apple, ed., *Cultural and Economic Reproduction in Education*, pp. 181-201.

[46]I have discussed the relationship between the commodification process and the dynamics of cultural capital at greater length in Apple, *Education and Power*.

[47]Ibid., especially chapter 5.

[48]A related argument is made in Douglas Kellner, "Network Television and American Society," *Theory and Society* 10 (January 1981): 31-62. See also Philip Wexler, "Structure, Text and Subject: A Critical Sociology of School Knowledge," in Apple, ed., *Cultural and Economic Reproduction in Education*, pp. 275-303.

[49]The relationship among deskilling, reskilling, and the sexual division of labor is treated in more depth in Michael W. Apple, "Work, Gender and Teaching," *Teachers College Record* 84 (Spring 1983): 611-628. See also David Gordon, Richard Edwards, and Michael Reich, *Segmented Work, Divided Workers: The Historical Transformation of Labor in the United States* (New York: Cambridge University Press, 1982).

[50]I do not want to imply that what is "transmitted" in schools is necessarily what is in the text. Nor do I want to claim at all that what is taught is wholly "taken in" by students. For analyses of teacher and student rejection, mediation, or transformation of the form and/or content of curriculum, see Paul Willis, *Learning to Labour* (Westmead, England: Saxon House, 1977); Robert Everhart, *Reading, Writing and Resistance* (Boston: Routledge and Kegan Paul, 1983); Michael W. Apple, "Work, Gender, and Teaching"; the chapters by Linda McNeil, Andrew Gitlin, and Lois Weis, in Apple and Weis, eds., *Ideology and Practice in Schooling*; and Carmen Luke, Suzanne Castell, and Alan Luke, "Beyond Criticism: The Authority of the School Text," *Curriculum Inquiry* 13 (Summer 1983): 111-127.

Chapter 6.
Curriculum and Technology

DECKER F. WALKER

W e live in a profoundly and incorrigibly technological society. Humanity's activities have so transformed earth that no modern civilization could be sustained without our agricultural, mechanical, chemical, transportation, communication, and medical technologies. In those corners where human impact is slight, such as parks, wilderness preserves, and undeveloped land, we explain that we have restrained ourselves, not that we lack the power to change them. The sea, fresh ground and surface waters, and the atmosphere have been profoundly affected by human activity, and it appears inevitable that their future composition will depend on our activities. To control or reduce the impact of human activities on earth would require more application of more sophisticated technology—miniaturized, refined, designed to do more with less.

Put simply, humanity now has the biblically promised dominion over the earth. We live in a managed environment. We may choose among forms of technology, provided several forms will serve our essential needs within the limitations to which we are subject, but we may not choose to avoid technology. We have no choice but to develop our technology to greater heights of sophistication and complexity.

Decker F. Walker is Associate Professor, School of Education, Stanford University, Stanford, California.

What This Means for Curriculum Thinking

Societies around the globe are being transformed by technology. The houses we live in, the jobs we hold, our patterns of social relationship, our life-styles, our institutions (families, businesses, courts, legislatures, churches) are being transformed by developments in transportation, manufacturing, communication, medicine, and agriculture. Think of the new social patterns that have emerged in just the last quarter-century: the prevalence of families shaped by divorce and remarriage; single-parent families, joint custody of children, step-parenting, two-income families, latch-key children, declining birth rates in developed nations, exploding population growth in developing nations; multi-national corporations, franchising, the failures of government regulation leading to the restructuring of the post office, the telephone system, and the banking system; the decline of traditional industries and the growth of automation, electronics, biotechnology, space technology; burgeoning employment in service industries; internationalization of commodities markets and financial dealings; the industrialization of farming; processed food; manufactured housing; shopping centers. What do such convulsive changes imply for what we teach the children of the 1980s?

The students we serve in school are affected by technology in ways that demand attention from curriculum theorists. They are children of the television age, now the video age. They come to school knowledgeable about the world, at least as portrayed on TV, and fluent in processing visual and auditory information, but confused about "what's really real." They have grown up plugged into electronic networks that offer them excitements not available at home or in school; media where their hopes and dreams, their fears and concerns, are expressed for their consumption by an industry and a culture— a child culture and an adolescent culture with its own heroes and villains, its own mores—tailored to and tailoring their tastes. Various anodynes—chemical, electronic, quasi-religious—are readily available to them. At the same time, the security provided by their families has eroded, leaving them vulnerable to extra-familial influences at an earlier age, and perhaps making them especially vulnerable to psychological disorders. In some ways, the children of the 1980s are more homogeneous, reflecting their exposure to the uniformities of the electronic media and the decline in influence of familial and ethnic factors. But since these trends have affected some children more than others, they come to us in some ways a more diverse lot than before. I find little in contemporary curriculum thought addressing the curricular implications of such technology-related changes in our students.

The various branches of knowledge are also being transformed. Scientific knowledge continues to explode at ever-increasing rates and, as it does, new relationships among phenomena turn up that blur and redraw the boundaries among disciplines: we learn that cosmology bears a close relationship to the high-energy physics of sub-atomic particles; physiology turns out to depend on molecular biochemistry, and genetics fits in there somewhere, too. The theory of information turns out to be applicable in genetics and psychology as well as in electrical engineering, and so on. As new disciplines become central in contemporary scholarly and scientific life, old foundation knowledge proves inadequate, and new foundations must be erected. The mathematics of continua which pervade our algebra, trigonometry, and geometry courses in the secondary school do not serve as well as foundations for the modern mathematical sciences as do topics in discrete mathematics—sets, probability, logic. Historians are rewriting history to take account of the influences of technology on past civilizations. And new skills become relevant, too—computer programming, keyboarding, word processing, data analysis. Even our conception of what qualifies as warranted knowledge is undergoing a challenge. Are mathematical proofs to be admitted which are so complicated that only computers can carry out and check the steps? Are theories so vague that they cannot be put in the form of a computer model to be regarded as too vague for scientific status?

Considered together, the transformations wrought by technology in the foundations of educational thought constitute, I think, the most powerful driving force for curriculum change in our time. If technology is having such a profound effect on the commonplaces of curriculum thought, surely we must give it serious attention in curriculum theory. Certainly it is possible for schools to ignore these developments and to preserve existing patterns of courses, topics, goals, and curriculum structures, as European schools have for a century largely ignored developments related to industrialism in their primary schools and their academically oriented secondary schools. American education has traditionally been more responsive to social trends, but this could be an exception.

What scant attention curriculum writers have given to technological issues has been polarized and partisan. On the one hand we find proposals being made to embrace a technological method of thinking about the curriculum (Bobbitt, Charters,[1] and the social efficiency advocates or their modern counterparts Popham, Mager,[2] and advocates of objectives-based curriculum design). On the other hand, we find critiques of the technological society coupled with propoals to use the schools as antidotes to its inhumane mechanism (Bode, Rugg,[3] the child-centered progressives, the social reconstructionists,

Kliebard, Apple, Huebner, the reconceptualists). All too often works of the
first type apply technological modes of thought simplistically and uncritically
to education, while works of the latter type claim technology has nothing to
add to the modes of thought inherited from the humanities. Neither an
uncritical embrace nor an uncritical rejection of technology will do. John
Dewey is the last prominent curriculum thinker to consider seriously and
critically the implications for education of the patterns of material life.[4] We
need another John Dewey, perhaps several, to interpret for us the social
changes we are undergoing and to help us think how best to prepare our
children for their futures in a technological society.

What sort of education should you and I, people of a technological society,
choose for ourselves and our children? This is the primary educational issue
of our time. It calls for the deepest thought about our world, our lives, and
our education. Such a question cannot be answered in a few pages, but I
would like to suggest some of the directions curriculum thinking might take
on this issue.

Who Should Be Educated?

A technological society needs leaders who understand technology—
leaders in politics, business, and finance, in law and the other professions, as
well as in the narrowly technical occupations. Therefore, most of those leaders
will need an excellent basic education in science and technology. The U.S.
has imported a substantial portion of its scientific and technically trained
leadership from Europe and the third world since World War II. But now
these societies are striving to build their own scientific and technical institutions. If the U.S. is to avoid draining the developed world of its precious talent,
we must send to our colleges and universities a much larger cohort of our
own young people with sound, thorough preparation for studying scientific
and technical subjects.

We also need thousands of qualified individuals equipped to deal with
the ever-growing complexity and differentiation of technical specialties. We
may be able to automate a certain amount of technical work, but this in itself
requires expertise. To secure a sufficiency of human intelligence trained to
work on our ever-broadening technical frontiers, it will be necessary for us
to extend the opportunity for such an education to every child.

The cognitive demands of formal subjects like science and mathematics
are high and severe. Mistakes are not matters of taste and are difficult to hide.
The work cannot be made arbitrarily easy because in the end the complexity
and subtlety of nature determines the difficulty of science and who knows

what determines the difficulty of mathematics. As a result, it is unlikely that every student will learn with the pace and facility required for success in advanced scientific and technical study. So, while we need virtually universal opportunity, we should not expect equality of results.

Thus, scientific, mathematical, and technical studies will continue to be competitive and meritocratic, and therefore at odds with our democratic and egalitarian ideals. On the other hand, if schools do not provide an opportunity for the pursuit of excellence in scientific and technical studies, then either the society will suffer the consequences of an inadequate pool of developed talent in this critical area or concerned individuals will find other ways to provide the necessary preparation outside school. Schools will need to cope with this tension between excellence and equality.

The largest pools of untapped technical talent in our society are women and minorities. Developing educational programs that attract women and minorities and enable them to succeed in scientific and technical studies is another curriculum challenge we need to face.

The high rate of growth and development of knowledge means that we cannot expect any individual to acquire enough knowledge in the first third of life to coast through the rest. Continuing education, recurrent education, education throughout the lifespan will be essential. The implications of this for schools are not clear. On the one hand, it suggests that schools need to provide a firm foundation for a lifetime of learning. On the other hand, it opens the possibility of letting difficult educational tasks slide until the students are more mature (and someone else's responsibility), and it relegates elementary and secondary schooling to the status of merely one phase of a larger process, merely one claimant among many for the society's educational resources.

What Should Be Taught?

The arguments in favor of deeper and more widespread learning of science and mathematics in elementary and secondary education are straightforward, but more than good arguments will be required to realize such an improvement. To be considered an educated person has never required more than a smattering of scientific and technical knowledge, if that. Our social and educational elite have not traditionally received a scientific or technical education. There are elective subjects in high school. In the university, all students are required to complete some courses in the cultural subjects, but few universities impose similar requirements to study science and mathematics on their nonscience majors. Language and the cultural subjects have been and remain the central defining characteristics of an educated person.

Realizing a change of this magnitude in social ideals entails a substantial transformation in the social status hierarchy. Either those at the top of our status pyramid have to change their values, re-educate themselves, and educate their children in a new way, or else they need to give way to individuals with different education and values. Such a transformation may be possible, may even be well under way, but, barring social upheaval, it is the work of centuries. In the meantime, the wealthy, business and financial leaders, entertainers, and sports figures rank higher in prestige, power, and income. Our children see this, too.

Other content may be equally or more deserving as preparation for life in a technological society. The pace and unpredictability of technological change argue for "learning to learn," emphasizing the learning of general principles and strategies that can be applied to a wide array of situations. Across the curriculum we should expect continued widespread interest in cultivating powers of discovery, invention, and research—the so-called higher-order cognitive skills. Stanley Pogrow in *Education in the Computer Age* argues that this is the primary imperative of a technological age.[5] In a similar vein, the authors of *No Limits to Learning* call for *innovative learning* as contrasted with maintenance learning, learning that would enable people to anticipate developments, prepare for them, and adapt quickly and well to changing circumstances.[6] They suggest that this type of learning requires more than simply cognitive skills and academic learning, however. They foresee a need for attention to values, to autonomy and integration both for individuals and for societies, to participation, and to human relations. In fact, the report *No Limits to Learning* does not even mention scientific and technical education as one of the priorities for an educational system of the future!

A knowledge of science and technology does not necessarily prepare one to adapt to or direct social change. For that, we will clearly need ways to deal in a more integrated fashion with the personal and social issues created by change. Substantial sectors of the public have consistently resisted efforts by public schools to address such personal and social-emotional issues, claiming that they should be handled by the family or church, but not by a secular, government-sponsored, tax-supported system of public schools. If the adjustments required grow more frequent and serious, some means must be found to help individuals adapt. The school will doubtlessly have some role to play in this process.

Various other bodies of content and skill may rise or decline in curricular importance for obvious reasons. Typing, if it remains the principal means of communication between people and computers, may become much more central. Spelling instruction may decline after the early years of schooling if computer programs that check spelling become widely used; using such a program is tantamount to having your own private spelling tutor every time you write. Those topics in mathematics that are most central to current applications—statistics, discrete mathematics, logic, and so forth—should become increasingly important. In general, a more equal emphasis is desirable between the skills of intellectual production and those of intellectual consumption; writing should become as important as reading; proving and applying mathematical results as important as comprehending them; designing and carrying out simple scientific investigations as important as interpreting scientific results.

We face a new dilemma in the case of purely formal knowledge—like arithmetic or the rudiments of a foreign language. Machines are already available that perform much better than any beginner and better than all but the best experts. Should we therefore discard these subjects from the curriculum, teach them in some new form (such as estimation and mental arithmetic), or continue to teach them for different reasons?

Why Educate?

The traditional mixture of motives for educating ourselves and our children will doubtlessly continue, but priorities may change. It should be clear from the foregoing discussion that economic motives for education are likely to loom larger in a technological society, unless the technological promise of abundance for all is realized.

The rationale for liberal education—education for its own sake, for awareness of the best that has been thought and said, for attaining a more complete humanity—is undermined by a scientific and technical education to the extent that it is pursued for vocational reasons alone. But liberal ideals of education can be reconciled with technical education. The responsibilities of managing our environment are fully as high a calling as those of citizenship traditionally defined. Buildings, bridges, highways, and machines are cultural artifacts as characteristically human and as worthy of study in their own way as poems, novels, plays, and paintings. Mathematics has beauty and power of expression just as does natural language. Undeniably, scientific and technical studies cannot fill the educational role of the humanities, but neither are they necessarily inconsistent with them. A good liberal education for life in a technological society will certainly contain more than a smattering of study in science, mathematics, and technology.

If we can generalize from those who participate most in the more scientific and technical aspects of today's society, prestige will be a major motivating force. Competition for prizes and honors and a place in the history books of one's discipline are the highest marks of distinction. Once again, we see competition and tension between achievement and equality, but this tension is also present among politicians struggling for power, business people for wealth, and artists for fame.

When the road to success appears to lie through learning, it is likely that those who reject the goal of material and secular success will reject the learning that brings it. Hence, instead of the most disaffected voices coming from a highly educated intellectual elite, as happens now, it is conceivable that the most disaffected groups in a scientific and technological society will reject education as then defined and embrace other ideals—courage, simplicity, sincerity, loyalty, honor, individuality, or love.

But none of these adult motives are terribly meaningful for most children. Disinterested curiosity is probably greater among children than adults, and the natural world, the man-made world, and the world of formal thought are all fruitful environments on which to exercise it. The desire to please parents and teachers will surely continue to carry weight. The desire for status in the peer group will continue to be important. If we expect children to study harder, longer, or better, we will need to be ingenious in developing ways to appeal to motives that are real for them, or else all our other curriculum planning may come to nothing.

When Will Education Take Place?

Clearly, education goes on throughout the life span. Preschool education already is an important non-public phase of education, and enrollment in post-secondary education approaches levels characteristic of secondary education as late as the 1930s. For some years now community colleges have been the fastest growing segment of the higher education system in the U.S. The accelerating pace of change makes obsolescence an ever-present danger in every endeavor, including pure science and mathematics as well as more mundane vocations. We are told to expect to have two or three "careers" in the course of our lifespan. All this will require re-education, continuing education, inservice education. In addition, with an aging population, the political support for adult education at public expense is likely to grow.

Where Will Education Take Place?

All these developments suggest that education will take place in many different environments in addition to traditional schools. This raises momentous issues concerning the school and its role as one educative institution among many in a technologically advanced society. One can imagine a narrow role for schools. They were invented for literacy training; that is still their primary role. Perhaps it should be their special educational function, leaving science, technical studies, the arts, and vocational subjects for other specialized educational institutions—perhaps clubs, community organizations, or specially designed youth groups sponsored by business and professional groups. If schools adopt such a narrow definition of their role, then science and technology will play but a minor part in them, except possibly as a medium or method of instruction, and the energies of educators concerned with science and technology will shift to the creation of specialized institutions. The implications of such a breakup of our monolithic school system are impossible to foresee, but one clear consequence could be a diminished role for the common school and the comprehensive school. Probably we would experience a period of institutional innovation with the eventual emergence of new educational institutions to take up scientific and technical education of young people.

A good case can be made for carrying on a significant amount of scientific and technical education in the workplace, where much of present technical preparation already takes place. Recent collaboration between universities and industry groups suggests that businesses may take on a larger role in such education. The need for constant updating of processes will necessitate retraining as much as retooling machinery. In industries that rely upon a high rate of innovation, work itself assumes a good deal of the character of education—research is conducted, seminars are held, presentations are given, training materials are produced and used, even the grounds resemble a college campus. College tuition is provided as a job benefit. Local colleges are invited to hold classes in company buildings.

Already various city, county, state, and federal agencies are heavily involved in education. In Palo Alto, the city-owned utility company conducts workshops on energy conservation; the department of parks and recreation conducts a full schedule of year-round classes; the court system provides drug education programs for drug-related misdemeanors, and driving school for traffic offenders. Nationally, the Department of Agriculture runs massive programs of education for farmers, and the Defense Department operates the largest school system in the world for its dependents, not to speak of the massive education and training efforts of the services for their personnel.

At home, "Sesame Street" and its counterparts provide literacy training. The British Open University offers a complete university in the home. Home computers hold out the promise of individualized tutoring. Perhaps the ultimate development in this direction is the possibility of networks of people educating one another via telecommunications. Such networks may make it possible for the establishment of learning communities, so that anyone anywhere may join and move up in sophistication at his or her own pace, keeping and changing "friends" along the way, helping and being helped, and feeling a part of an extended community built around shared interests. Will such developments make the home a prominent locus for education again? Perhaps so, but only if adults stay home. Present trends would have all the adults at work.

Providing education in many locales complicates the problem of monitoring progress and coordinating efforts. In many ways the first grade teacher's job is easier if all children arrive more or less equally ignorant and unskilled. When they instead demonstrate intricate and varied patterns of attainment and ignorance, carrying on group instruction becomes difficult. There will be a greater need for methods of assessing individuals' knowledge for proper placement into the plethora of learning situations. Regulations will be needed to assure fair access to them.

How Will This Education Be Carried On?

Education is likely to increasingly take place via recorded media, in a self-service mode, and with the help of near-peers. Such arrangements make education less costly, more flexible in time and place, and less cumbersome institutionally. Traditional forms of live instruction will not disappear, but newer forms of instruction will arise. The situation is similar to that in housing. Economics dictate cheaper, mass-produced housing, but tradition stands in the way, so the new forms (mobile homes) are introduced among those who cannot afford to aspire to the accepted standard. Gradually the homes improve and more of us find ourselves priced out of the conventional home market, and thus the new form will gain acceptance. Similarly, in technical and military training, we find growing reliance on media and self-study materials. One finds similar developments in test-preparation courses such as those for the SAT.

Conclusion

I think the greatest challenge these developments pose for schools is institutional adaptation. All social change is stressful for schools because schools are universal institutions charged to serve the children of those who want change and those who resist it. To ignore social change places schools at risk of irrelevance. Schools are already perceived as removed from social reality (witness talk of schoolboy illusions and ivory towers). Too much distance and they lose public support. On the other hand, making major changes is difficult and risky, too. As governmental institutions, schools are obliged to follow the mandates of elected officials, and governmental direction is notoriously slow and undependable. Schools are also bound by contracts with their teachers which prevent them from restructuring themselves to meet the challenges of a changing environment. In short, public elementary and secondary schools are both slow and difficult to change. Yet technological developments are transforming the society the schools serve, and the schools cannot afford to ignore these changes. This is a cruel dilemma, but one that must be faced.

I have been following developments in the use of computer technology in schools fairly closely for the past five years, and what I have seen there highlights the dilemma. On the one hand, schools have responded heroically to the challenge of the microcomputer. Most secondary schools and many elementary schools have established computer centers and offer a completely new school subject—computer programming. This has been done with little formal teacher training, almost no reliance on the base budget, and with the enthusiastic support of many parents. This must certainly rank as one of the most improbable achievements of educational innovation. By comparison, enormous effort has been expended for decades to gain acceptance of economics as a school subject.

On the other hand, these achievements fall far short of what the society needs, of what other institutions have been able to provide, and of what computer advocates have demonstrated can be done. Only a few students in most secondary schools have any contact with computers at school; in a sample of five Bay Area high schools I studied in the spring of 1982, only 13 percent of students reported using computers at school, whereas more than twice as many reported experience with computers outside school. The dreams of such visionaries as Patrick Suppes and Seymour Papert have been realized in experimental settings, but few schools even approach these ideals. Mostly schools are struggling to teach computer literacy and programming in BASIC or Logo. I can easily find special locations in the Bay Area where a child could learn much more about computers than in the public elementary and secondary schools—the Exploratorium, Lawrence Hall of Science, and the Institute for Computer Technology, for example.

Schools have responded to the microcomputer revolution with unprecedented (for them) speed and thoroughness, especially in such lean times. Yet what they have accomplished is utterly inadequate. To devote more resources to this activity would require diverting them from other activities or raising additional revenues, both slow and difficult alernatives. Schools are already under fire from inside and out for what they are now doing and for not doing enough. The average age of teachers in the Bay Area high schools I studied was 49. While they were favorably inclined toward computers and wanted to learn more about them, they nonetheless have a considerable investment in their present practices, and many have little incentive to change beyond curiosity. I cannot resist the impression that despite wonderful intentions and as great an effort as they can muster, schools are fumbling the ball on the use of computers. They will never be able to succeed in changing their curriculum as quickly and thoroughly as reformers outside schools can do, and, if they should succeed, they face criticism from those who resist the change.

Just as we cannot turn back from technology but can only redirect it in the future, so we will not, I think, be able to insulate schools from these developments. Even if we could, we should not want to. Curriculum theorists can ignore these developments or attack them or analyze them, but our highest professional duty demands that we help schools to build curriculums for our time. Life sets us this challenge. Let us face it and build the best world we can under the circumstances. This is what Benjamin Franklin, Horace Mann, and John Dewey all did in their times. We honor them best not by preserving the educational forms they created but by following their example and helping to create ones better suited to our own time.

Notes

[1] Franklin W. Bobbitt, *The Curriculum* (Boston: Houghton Mifflin Co., 1918); and William W. Charters, *The Curriculum* (New York: Macmillan, 1923).

[2] James Popham, *Instructional Objectives* (Chicago: Rand McNally, 1969); and Robert Mager, *Preparing Instructional Objectives* (Belmont, Calif.: Fearon, 1975).

[3] Boyd Bode, *Modern Educational Theories* (New York: Macmillan, 1927); and Harold Rugg and Ann Shoemaker, *The Child-Centered School* (Yonkers, N.Y.: World Book, 1928).

[4] Dewey's earliest statements, for example, "My Pedagogic Creed," *School Journal* LIV (1897), show his concern for "forms of community life," which include the extended communality of production and consumption and the technology thereof.

[5] Stanley Pogrow, *Education in the Computer Age* (Beverly Hills, Calif.: Sage, 1983).

[6] James W. Botkin, *No Limits to Learning* (New York: Pergamon Press, 1979).

Chapter 7.
Qualitative and Aesthetic Views of Curriculum and Curriculum Making

VINCENT R. ROGERS

A few years ago I was asked to review a new piece of educational research by the *London Times Educational Supplement*.[1] The study dealt with a comparison of formal, mixed, and informal methods in English primary schools, and its basic conclusion was that "basic subjects" are taught more effectively in formal rather than in informal classrooms. The study, Neville Bennett's *Teaching Styles and Pupil Progress*,[2] received an enormous amount of coverage in the British press and on radio and television. In addition, Bennett's results were almost instantaneously (and, one suspects, joyously) picked up by the American media, with coverage by everyone from CBS's Dan Rather to the Hartford (Connecticut) *Courant*.

It would be impossible to overestimate the effects of the Bennett study. The results were released at a time of national frustration with a variety of gnawing, perplexing problems: the legacy of Vietnam and Watergate; the "new ethnicity" with its strident cry for Black Power, Brown Power, and Red Power; urban riots; affirmative action; the passing of Public Law 94-142 and its implications for the education of the handicapped, to name only a few. Frustrated and angry, confused and seemingly powerless to deal with this tidal wave of social, economic, and political change, many Americans turned their attention to the schools as a possible source of the nation's difficulties.

The Bennett study was exquisitely well timed. It said what many wanted to hear; it concluded that more "progressive," student-centered education

Vincent R. Rogers is Professor of Education, University of Connecticut, Storrs.

had failed; what the nation needed was a return to a more formal, teacher-directed, "no-nonsense" kind of schooling.

The *London Times* took the precaution of publishing Bennett's results along with four more objective reviews of his work (mine and those of three British writers), which added a degree of balance to their coverage that was noticeably absent elsewhere. For the most part, and with the exception of the *New York Times*, the British and American media handled the story by presenting Bennett's damning conclusions as a matter of scientific fact, without a hint of critical reaction.

I have no wish to report in detail the methodological faults I found in Bennett's work. Nevertheless, it seems important to summarize my major criticisms as proper and appropriate background for much that is to follow:

● There is no evidence that the children in the formal, informal, and mixed classrooms were of equal ability.

● There is no evidence that the children were of similar socioeconomic backgrounds. And that, of course, is of enormous importance since it is generally agreed among virtually all researchers that socioeconomic class is the single most accurate predictor of success or failure in school.

● Fifty percent of the teachers who took part in the study agreed that the tests favored formal teaching.

● There is no evidence that the formal and informal teachers had equal amounts of teaching experience; however, there is some indication that the formal teachers were considerably more experienced.

● Bennett makes the incorrect assumption, without substantiating evidence, that all children in formal classrooms were treated identically, as were all children in informal classrooms.

● A careful analysis of Bennett's data shows that the great variability within groups and excessive overlap between groups makes the reported differences of little or no practical significance.

● Five of the 12 formal classes took the 11+ examination during the experimental year, while only three of the 13 informal classes took the examination. The 11+ examination does have an impact on three Rs scores, yet this variable is uncontrolled in the study.

● Imaginative writing was assessed through the formal assignment of the topic "invisibility" to all children—a procedure that violates virtually everything we know about encouraging creative responses in children.

● It is generally agreed that in a study of this type we are primarily concerned with the effects of teaching styles on the scores of class. ooms of children rather than on individual children. We are not concerned with a direct comparison between John in a formal classroom, and David in an informal classroom. Instead, we are asking if the average of the children in the 12 formal classrooms, considered as 12 groups, is different from the average of children in the 13 informal classrooms, also considered as groups. Thus the appropriate unit of analysis used is the number of classrooms (37), not the number students (950). That is an essential point, since it is a great deal easier to obtain significant statistical differences when one uses a large unit of analysis. It is interesting to contemplate the change that might occur in Bennett's results if the correct unit of analysis had been used.

• Bennett's global conclusions about the effectiveness of formal teaching often mask the results of his own data. For example, he concludes in the section devoted to reading that "the results provide clear evidence for the better performance of formal and mixed pupils." Even if we were to accept Bennett's statistical procedures, we find that formal methods were ineffective with lower achieving boys, and that virtually no differences existed among girls at any level—except for the low achieving girls, for whom, paradoxically, formal methods seemed more effective. If one also considers the statistical and methodological problems outlined above, it is clear that the evidence is extremely uncertain.

The issues I have raised here are vitally important to any teacher, parent, or principal who would consider changing the schools on the basis of such research. Moreover, each criticism listed has been substantiated by a number of British research scholars, including a scathing critique of Bennett's study that appeared recently in the British *Journal of Educational Research*.[3]

I've used the Bennett study as a symbol of one of the most pressing problems we face in American education. His research was eagerly read and quickly accepted as "fact," partially because it said what many people wanted to hear, and partially because it was couched in the language of what Guba[4] calls "conventional inquiry." Bennett writes of means, standard deviations, null hypotheses, statistically significant differences, matched groups, and controlled variables—language that suggests accuracy, objectivity, and authority. It has become the conventional research wisdom of our time.

As I examined this phenomenon, I attempted to identify the assumptions that underlie current approaches to curriculum evaluation in the schools. That is, in order to accept the methods of "conventional inquiry," what must one believe? What are the underlying assumptions that dictate the nature of curriculum evaluation in our schools? What do most professionals seem to believe? What can we infer about such beliefs from a study of the nature of the mode of curriculum inquiry which so dominates our schools?

The following list, while certainly not inclusive, suggests some of the most common assumptions that guide the evaluation process in most of our schools.

1. Linguistic modes of learning and expression are the only modes of learning worth evaluating. Thus, we place great value on using words to name, describe, or define, while placing minimum value on visual, auditory, and kinesthetic modes of reacting to phenomena.

2. Learning can be assessed piecemeal, at any given moment in time, without concern for learning over long periods of time.

3. "Efficiency" is of primary importance in the teaching-learning act, that is, we are most concerned with how early and how fast something can be learned.

4. Learning takes place in certain formal settings such as classrooms, libraries, and laboratories.

5. Grades and test scores give a reasonable picture of school performance.

6. What we see or measure now is likely to be a stable characteristic over time.

7. Testing conditions have no important effects on the teaching-learning situation, that is, administering an "objective test" has neutral effects on the learner.

8. What is learned or experienced in one field has no effect on what is experienced in other fields.

9. Evidence obtained through direct observation of or interaction with the learner is inferior to that obtained in two dimensional "tests."

10. The learner's products, poems, sketches, models, and so forth are of relatively minor value in the evaluative process.

11. The processes used in coming to a problem's solution are not as important as the answer.

12. The content of most subjects taught, their basic ideas and concepts, as well as the material used to teach them, are of significance and therefore worth teaching.

13. The personal qualities of teachers are neutral and have little effect on learning.

14. The accumulation of a number of specific skills or segments of subject matter will eventually add up to a coherent whole.

15. Learning can always be demonstrated in some overt, observable way.

16. Various curriculums within a given field (for example, four or five competing elementary school science textbooks series) have similar

goals and content and can therefore be evaluated by using standardized tests.

17. Objectives must be stated clearly before evaluation can take place.
18. The judgment and perception of the evaluator are not to be trusted.
19. Evaluation is an integral part of data gathering. In other words, methodology concludes with a judgmental statement; a new curriculum or method has been successful or has failed in terms of a given set of criteria.

While it may be awkward, even embarrassing, to admit that these propositions largely govern curriculum evaluation, any reasonable, objective analysis of existing curriculum research reveals that this is indeed the case. In fact, the 1982-83 volume of the *Journal of Education Research* published 56 studies in all. Of this total, 45 could be described as using the methods of "conventional inquiry" while only 11 used alternative modes.

While some educational theorists and a few practitioners are aware of the increasing interest in more naturalistic, qualitative means of curriculum evaluation, conventional inquiry continues to dominate the field.

So far I have tried to explain why certain practices are used so extensively in curriculum evaluation and educational research in general. Given the foregoing set of assumptions, these procedures must follow inevitably.

There is, of course, nothing inherently wrong with all of this; one believes what one believes and then acts accordingly. It should be clear to the perceptive reader, however, that an alternate set of assumptions is implied by the original list. If, for example, an original assumption suggests that the effects of informal educational settings are ignored, an obvious corollary is that the study of informal settings is of great importance and often reveals subtle insights about the subjects' behavior.

In which direction, then, do we go? Bennett's study was timely and important. It dealt with matters of considerable methodological and curricular significance. I rejected it, however, not only because of its technical flaws, but also because, flawed or not, the fundamental mode of inquiry he chose to investigate so complex a phenomenon is inadequate for the job.

I would have preferred to have Bennett study these schools over a considerably longer period of time; I would have preferred that he had used many types of evidence to describe what children were learning in schools; I would have preferred that he and his colleagues spend more hours on site observing children, teachers, parents, and administrators face-to-face. And I would have preferred that he resist the temptation to praise or condemn on the basis of data so flawed and incomplete.

In short, I would have preferred that he use many of the methods we associate with what we have come to call qualitative or naturalistic inquiry.

I have described this method extensively elsewhere.[5] Nevertheless, let me underscore the fundamental concepts that seem to form the foundations for these approaches to curriculum research and evaluation.

Qualitative researchers believe that:

1. Any social entity or institution is enormously complex and subtle. It is difficult to understand what is happening in a first grade reading group or a middle-school classroom. The experiences and attitudes of teachers and children both in and out of the school setting all have a bearing on what occurs within the classroom or school. Qualitative researchers accept these complexities, believing that only through their unraveling will anything resembling accurate description result.

2. Intensive study of a given phenomenon over a long period of time is essential for genuine understanding of that phenomenon. Teaching and learning are ongoing processes constantly in flux; to understand what is happening requires sustained, longitudinal study.

3. People and institutions must be studied holistically, and not in isolation from other forces that may influence them. The "wholes" or units may vary in size and complexity, and it may be necessary to study many "wholes" before accurate description of a larger unit emerges. Nevertheless, what goes on in the cafeteria or art studio is indeed related to what goes on elsewhere, both within and outside of the school. The qualitative researcher studies all related and relevant phenomena.

4. The most effective way to study a given phenomenon is through direct, on-site, face-to-face contact with people and events in question. What people do is often different from what they say. Thus, reliance on paper and pencil tests and questionnaires is often misleading. Rosenthal and Jacobson's classic study, *Pygmalion in the Classroom* (1968) suggested that teachers' expectations bring about dynamic changes in their judgment of children's work. Yet we know little about what actually happened in such classrooms—how teachers treated children, how children responded to such treatment. Only first-hand observation would reveal such subtleties.

5. Knowledge of the behavior of human beings in a given social context is relatively meaningless without some understanding of the meanings those observed give to their behavior. Thus the qualitative researcher seeks to understand the attitudes, values, beliefs, and underlying assumptions of those being studied, to understand how others view their world. High school students may indeed join informal groups or cliques in school, but such information is relatively useless unless we know why students choose to associate

with one group rather than another, or what their perceptions are of the values and purposes of such groups. At another level, a field trip to the zoo may be seen by the principal as a learning experience that expands the conventional curriculum. The teacher may view it as "a breather," a day away from the "drudgery of daily classroom life."

6. The basic function of the researcher is *description*; the richest, fullest, most comprehensive description possible. Such "thick description" enables the researcher to perceive subtleties in human behavior (is a raised eyebrow a conscious reaction or merely a twitch?) that are vital to full understanding. Such description suggests a basic interest in process rather than product or output. Qualitative researchers describe but do not judge or evaluate—although their data may well be used by others in an evaluative sense. Thus a school may richly document the lives of children as they move through school, including samples of children's work, excerpts from teachers' and children's journals, comments of observers, and so on. Parents, teachers, and others concerned with the quality of children's schooling must then assess this "thick description" and decide for themselves on the adequacy of the school's programs, methods, and activities.

This last point seems to me to be absolutely vital in importance. Clearly, the notion of emphasizing description rather than evaluation or judgment (describing "how" rather than "how well") has its roots in anthropological inquiry. However, this notion seems to have spawned a new breed of evaluation specialists in education who, in fact, have developed models designed to describe curricular and methodological events as richly and fully as possible; to reveal the fullness and subtlety that transpires in and out of classrooms so that decision makers can make the most informed decisions possible. Consider these examples:

1. *Prospect School's Documentation Model.*[6] Documentation as practiced in Prospect School consists of the gathering and analysis of a wealth of descriptive material on individual children collected longitudinally. Samples of children's painting, drawing, building, and other three-dimensional work, and writing as well as teacher observations, journals, and other material serve as the basis for the documentation process. These documents provide an in-depth description of the ways in which children become involved with materials, the nature of their interaction with adults and children, their interests, learning styles, and academic strengths and weaknesses.

Thus, through sampling the program in all its complexity, over time, and through the points of view of all the persons participating in it, the interested reader is provided with a biographical, historical account of the program that is not directly evaluative. Indeed, the program (or the work of a given child) can be evaluated by any standard that the evaluator wishes to apply.

2. *Elliot Eisner's Connoisseurship Model.* Educational connoisseurship is the "art of appreciation."[7] That is, the connoisseur, whether of wine, tennis, theater, or education, is able to see subtleties and nuances of his or her field of specialty. The educational connoisseur is able to observe, record, and describe events occurring in schools and classrooms more completely, more fully, and more meaningfully than is the neophyte. Connoisseurship skills are developed over time, through experience, and through practice. Educational criticism, as Eisner sees it, is the ability to illuminate, render, or disclose what has occurred in an educational setting—"to enable others to experience what they may have missed."[8]

These thick descriptions, written by trained educational critics, then become the subject for dialogue and discussion by teachers and other interested parties. Educational criticism would typically include not only the artistic description of events, however. Critics would raise questions such as, "Why is it that this classroom functions in this particular way? Why do these side effects occur? How does the reward structure of this classroom shape the relationships students have with one another? How is time used in this classroom?" Ultimately, evaluative issues are raised by both the critic and subject. The purpose, however, is not to evaluate on some normative basis, but rather to examine the nature of the match between what was intended and what transpired.

3. *Sara Lawrence Lightfoot's "Portraiture" Model.* Lightfoot[9] uses the term portraiture to describe her work because it allows maximum freedom from the traditions and constraints of conventional research. For Lightfoot, "portraiture" consists of relatively short (five or six days) intense visits to schools by experienced, skilled observers with years of research training. The researcher's purpose is to attempt to capture the school's "life, rhythm, and rituals" by uncovering the insider's view of what is important. Data sources include observational records, interviews, and the school's written documents; for example, school newspapers, literary journals, yearbooks, school catalogues, and attendance and other records.

As the research proceeds, significant themes are identified, often dealing with issues such as teacher autonomy, the quality of leadership, curricular strengths and weaknesses, and student values. These persistent themes are then made available for study and discussion by the actors in the play, the teachers, principals, students, and parents.

4. *Robert Stake's Responsive Model.*[10] Responsive evaluation also emphasizes portrayal rather than analysis. This approach recognizes the importance

of conditions that preceded a given curricular change, the ways in which the new program is being taught and learned as seen through the eyes of participants, and the program's outcomes, both intended and unintended.

Responsive evaluators "collect judgments" of all of the significant participants (children, teachers, and principals) rather than imposing their own views.

The evaluation begins with an extensive data base. However, a systematic form of reduction takes place as the study proceeds, so that the scope of the evaluation is continually narrowed. Thus unique and unpredicted events will also have a chance to be considered as the evaluation proceeds.

Ultimately, a responsive evaluation should sharpen discussion, disentangle complexities, isolate the significant from the trivial, and raise the level of sophistication of debate.

5. *Robert Wolfe's Judicial Mode.*[11] This model brings the technique of a court of law to educational evaluation. Essentially the judicial model is an educational hearing. Unlike a court of law, its goal is to provide a setting for the consideration of alternative arguments concerning a specific issue, rather than to "win a case."

The model proceeds through four identifiable stages: issue generation, issue selection, preparation of arguments, and the hearing itself.

As with other alternative evaluation models we have discussed, the judicial model makes extensive use of more subjective data (such as data gained through unstructured open-ended interviews with a diverse group of participants) and a continuing process of reduction of data so that the most significant issues and questions may be identified for discussion at "the hearing."

Thus, the eventual and culminating hearing becomes a forum for competing ideas in which witnesses present "evidence" and are questioned and asked to clarify or explain. Eventually a balanced account of the issue under question is given, and a more informed decision is ultimately made.

These new directions in evaluation have had an increasing effect on our work at the University of Connecticut. Our students have become deeply involved in descriptive research that we feel can and will make a significant difference to practitioners. This research follows no specific descriptive model (Eisner, Lightfoot, Stake, or others), but rather is eclectic in approach, using a variety of descriptive methods that are appropriate for the problem under study. Some of the most significant of the Connecticut studies include these:

• Chris Stevenson[12] was interested in the nature of the transition of 25 adolescents (ages 14-19) from a child-centered elementary school to a variety of types of conventional, traditional secondary schools. Each student was interviewed at considerable depth in order to arrive at what Stevenson calls the "essence" of their values and beliefs concerning the significance and impact of the school's formal and informal curriculum, the nature of their elementary schooling, secondary schooling, and the transition itself.

● Kay Doost[13] made use of the magnificent collection of student documents stored in the Prospect Archives at the Prospect School in Bennington, Vermont, to study aspects of the development of a single child's thinking over a period of eight years as well as the relationship of various curricular experiences to the child's intellectual growth. She examined samples of the child's writing, painting, drawing, work with clay, number work, participation in classroom activities, friendship patterns, and so on.

● Ann McGreevy[14] identified nine pairs of identical and fraternal twins, one of whom was selected for a special gifted/talented program in school while the other twin was not selected. She was interested in the effects of being included or rejected as perceived by the twins themselves, parents, and teachers, and in the nature of the curriculum each twin experienced as a member of a contrasting program. Her methodology included interviews, classroom observations, document analysis, and projective techniques.

● Karen Berg[15] wanted to identify parents' values as she embarked upon a curriculum revision project at the University Nursery School. She believed that parent support was essential to effective curriculum, and thus parent views must be sought. On the other hand, what parents say they will support may not be consistent with the values they have internalized and which motivate their actions. Berg used a phenomenological methodology to examine parents' views. Through in-depth, unstructured interviews, she involved parents in discussions of their preferences and concerns for their child's schooling; their satisfactions, disappointments and goals relative to their own education; and their methods of teaching children practical skills in the home.

● Kay Merriam[16] wanted to investigate what she called the "Latent Development of Outstanding Abilities," of recognized, outstanding adults in a number of fields whose abilities went largely *unrecognized* in childhood. She identified five individuals—a nuclear scientist; an outstanding environmentalist; an established, nationally known, multi-talented artist; a state governor; and an award-winning veterinary pathologist. She conducted oral history interviews with each individual, focusing on their experience at work, with mentors, peers, and parents, and particularly on the nature of their curricular and other school experiences.

● Camille Allen[17] was interested in describing the nature of social interaction occurring among a group of 4th, 5th, and 6th grade students and their teacher when a microcomputer was introduced into the classroom environment. Videotapes, participant observations, student logs, and structured interviews were her basic data sources. She identified the quality, types, and characteristics of social interaction between the teacher and her class.

• Karen List[18] wanted to identify educational and societal influences on the creative development of a group of outstanding young female artists. She conducted in-depth interviews with each of the 11 women in her study, analyzing the data both as a series of individual case studies and as a source of collective data. Thus individual portraits of each artist emerged, as did an overall picture of the curricular and other forces that effected their creative growth both in and out of schools.

Other, similar studies have been completed recently at the University of Connecticut: Speck's[19] study of perseverance or stick-to-itiveness in young gifted children; Arnold's[20] study of the thinking of four outstanding curricular theorists working in the field of early adolescent education; Sylcox's[21] study of older creative individuals; Kupperman's[22] study of the day-to-day activities of a building principal over an extended period of time; Story's[23] study of the characteristics of successful teachers of young gifted children; Rogers'[24] study of the out-of-school time use of children in a suburban, upper middle class community, and Rogers'[25] study of teacher and student perceptions of the effectiveness of a high school sex education curriculum.

I began this chapter by criticizing Neville Bennett's research, wishing he had studied his schools for a longer period of time, included a broader spectrum of evidence, spent more time on site observing children and classrooms, and examined the perceptions of children, teachers, parents, and other significant "actors in the play."

It should be clear that the models identified earlier in this chapter, including documentation, portraiture, connoisseurship, and so forth, have had their influence on curriculum thinking in a very practical way at the University of Connecticut. Our students (and students at other universities as well as teachers and administrators working in schools) have examined a number of important educational questions in ways that break out of the conventional research paradigm described earlier in this chapter. Clearly qualitative/aesthetic researchers have adopted a new set of assumptions to guide their work—assumptions which should lead to a deeper understanding of children, teachers, curriculum, and schooling in general.

What, then, can teachers and administrators do in a practical way to carry out the ideas discussed in this chapter? Is there anything one can realistically do, given the everyday survival pressures most teachers and administrators face? I think so.

We might begin by recognizing the value of a variety of kinds of data—including children's writing, drawing, poems, and sketches—as valuable evidence of children's performance.

In addition, and more specifically, I offer the following suggestions:

1. The Prospect School in Bennington, Vermont, offers workshops for teachers and administrators at Bennington and in addition will send teams of experienced practitioners to school districts wishing to learn more about the documentation process referred to in this chapter. I have also worked closely with a number of other schools in the greater Connecticut area that have developed innovative evaluative devices. I think particularly of the Mead School in Byram, the Whitby School in Greenwich, and the Early Learning Center in Stamford. One might also get in touch with Central Park East School in New York City, the Shoreham/Wading River Middle School in Shoreham, New York, and Thayer High School in Winchester, New Hampshire. Teachers and administrators at all of these schools have evolved alternative modes of evaluation.

2. Much of the work described in this chapter is the result of collaboration between my graduate students at the University of Connecticut and local school districts. Those districts have identified problems and we have worked directly with them to develop alternative data-gathering devices and, in fact, to gather much of the data itself. Similar collaborations might be arranged in other areas. In addition, a colleague in the educational administration department and I teach a course which involves the collaboration of a class of ten graduate students and three school districts in a program aimed at a better definition of the teaching/learning act.

The following excerpts are from a letter mailed to a number of Connecticut school superintendents. It described the course in some detail:

> During the first six weeks of the course, our graduate students would be trained to write broad educational "portraits" or "criticisms" based on the work of Elliot Eisner and Sara Lawrence Lightfoot. Our students will also study how to conduct effective interviews with teachers and children, how to analyze relevant educational documents such as curriculum guides, statements of goals and objectives, and lesson plans, and how to video-tape day-to-day life in classrooms.
>
> Six weeks of the course will then be devoted to data gathering in the schools. We would need approximately three classrooms from each participating school for clinical observations. Teachers who might be interested in having their instructions observed would be invited to a meeting at which the projects, goals and procedures would be explained and discussed. Then they would be asked to volunteer. There would be no pressure to participate.
>
> We would anticipate three, two-hour observations in each of three classrooms during the six weeks of "Clinical Sessions." In addition, those teachers observed will be interviewed concerning their perceptions of their work. Stu-

dents will also be interviewed so that students' perceptions become a part of the classroom "portrait." Our students will also analyze participating teachers' lesson plans, school curriculum guides, philosophical statements of purpose, and so forth.

During this phase of the course, we will attempt to describe or characterize these classrooms, to identify their pervasive qualities.

Data gathered during these sessions will be analyzed, organized and shared in seminar with participating teachers, administrators, and other teachers as deemed appropriate. The purpose of these seminars is to gain a deeper understanding of the teaching and learning act itself rather than to evaluate a given teacher.

As teachers discuss the university team's data they may wish to have narrower, more focused studies of specific aspects of their teaching. If so, the university team will develop appropriate techniques (including video-taping) for such followup.

As a result of these activities, we hope that both our students and participating teachers and administrators will have developed a number of more effective ways of examining the complex phenomenon we call teaching. How these techniques are eventually used in any given school will of course depend upon the needs and interests of that school.

Those interested in more information about the course and its content might write to me at the University of Connecticut.

3. A number of universities across the U.S. are doing exciting work in the area of qualitative research. I think particularly of Stanford University in Palo Alto, California, the University of Pennsylvania, and Cornell University, as well as a number of others. It would be wise to find out what is being offered at nearby colleges and universities and seek the help of faculty specializing in the application of these techniques to educational settings.

A particularly exciting example is a workshop offered by the University of Vermont titled, "Understanding the Curriculum of the Mind." Consider the following excerpts from the workshop description:

Curriculum evaluation in schools is generally carried out by examining conventional data such as student performance on norm and criterion-referenced tests and subjective expressions of teacher opinion regarding the merits of particular syllabi and published instructional materials. While this data is often useful, it does not adequately assess the more longitudinal and impressionistic outcomes of classroom experience. This institute is designed to cultivate teachers' and administrators' interests and skills for more comprehensive assessment of student learnings derived from existing curricula.

The outcome of school programs that should ultimately be of greatest interest to educators, however, is "the curriculum of the mind:" the complex of recollections, associations, impressions, interpretations, ideas and values that endure in a phenomenological context for each person. Virtually nothing is done in schools to understand this dimension of the school experience, and only recently have a few educators begun to explore it. What is "known" and endures as "knowledge" invites systematic exploration. This institute will provide a collegial setting lasting over several months for such study.

4. Inservice sessions might be used to foster the role of teacher as "naturalistic inquirer." That is, time spent in inservice programs might well be spent on helping teachers to become better data gatherers and better analyzers and interpreters of what goes on in classroom situations.

5. It would be most helpful if educational professionals would try to inform parents of the complexity of the educational process by using illustrative data of the kind described in this chapter. One of the problems most of us face is that the general public has a simplistic view of the teaching/learning act. It is quite possible that the careful use of the sort of material I have emphasized would help to convey this idea.

6. School districts might embark upon relatively simple follow-up studies of children moving from elementary into junior high schools and from junior to senior high schools. That is, it would be immediately useful and practical to understand children's views of the educational experiences they have had at a given level.

I don't suggest that any of this is simple. Nevertheless it is possible. Indeed everything I have discussed here is being done somewhere by teachers and administrators in American public schools.

Notes

[1]Vincent Rogers, "What the Polls Don't Tell Us About Education," *Principal* 56, 5 (May/June 1977): 43, 44.

[2]Neville Bennett, *Teaching Styles and Pupil Progress* (London: Open Books, 1976).

[3]John Gray and David Saterlee, "A Chapter of Errors: Teaching Styles and Pupil Progress in Retrospect," *British Journal of Educational Research* 19 (1976): 45-46.

[4]Egon Guba, *Toward a Methodology of Naturalistic Inquiry in Educational Evaluation* (Los Angeles: Center for the Study of Evaluation, UCLA, 1978).

[5]Vincent Rogers, "Qualitative Research: Another Way of Knowing," in *Using What We Know About Teaching*, ed. Philip L. Hosford (Alexandria, Va.: ASCD, 1984 Yearbook), pp. 87-88.

[6]Further information on documentation is available from The Director, Prospect School, Bennington, Vt.

[7]Elliot Eisner, *The Educational Imagination* (New York: Macmillan Publishing Co., 1979), p. 193.

[8]Ibid., p. 194.

[9]Sara Lawrence Lightfoot, *The Good High School* (New York: Basic Books, Inc., 1983).

[10]Robert Stake, "Program Evaluation: Responsers Evaluation," Occasional Paper No. 5, The Evaluation Center, Western Michigan University, 1975.

[11]R. L. Wolf, "Trial By Jury: A New Evaluation Method," *Phi Delta Kappan* (1975): 185-187.

[12]Christopher Stevenson, "A Phenomenological Study of Perceptions About Open Education Among Graduates of the Fayreweather Street School" (doctoral dissertation, University of Connecticut, 1979).

[13]Kay Doost, "A Child As Thinker: One Child's Thought As It Reflects Intentionality" (doctoral dissertation, University of Connecticut, 1979).

[14]Ann M. McGreevy, "A Study of Twins Included and Not Included in Gifted Programs" (doctoral dissertation, University of Connecticut, 1984).

[15]Karen Berg, "Enlisting Parental Endorsement for Curriculum Change: A Practical Model" (master's thesis, University of Connecticut, 1983).

[16]Kay Merriam, "Latent Development of Outstanding Abilities in Adults" (doctoral dissertation, University of Connecticut, 1984).

[17]Camille Ann Allen, "An Analysis of Social Interactions Among A Teacher and Small Groups of Students Working with Microcomputers" (doctoral dissertation, University of Connecticut, 1984).

[18]Karen Louise List-Ostroff, "A Study of Creative Women's Development Patterns through Age Thirty-Five" (doctoral dissertation, University of Connecticut, 1983).

[19]Angela Maria Tosto Speck, "The Task Commitment of Young Gifted Children: A Micro-Ethnographic Study of Teacher and Peer Behavior on Creative Productivity" (doctoral dissertation, University of Connecticut, 1984).

[20]John Fjoyd Arnold, "Open Education in the Middle Years (ages 10-15): An Analysis of the Thought of Roy Illsley, Charity James, Eugene Ruth and Donald Wells" (doctoral thesis, University of Connecticut, 1980).

[21]Karol Sylcox, "Creativity Among the Elderly" (doctoral dissertation in progress, University of Connecticut, 1984).

[22]Joel Kupperman, "Administrative Perspective: Study of a Secondary School Principal" (doctoral dissertation, University of Connecticut, 1983).

[23]Carol Mary Story, "Facilitator of Learning: A Micro-Ethnographic Study of the Teacher of the Gifted" (doctoral dissertation, University of Connecticut, 1984).

[24]Vincent Rogers, "Out of School Time Use" (unpublished paper, University of Connecticut, 1984).

[25]Vincent Rogers, Kay Merriam, and Michelle Munson, "Sex Education—Curriculum Issues," *Journal of Research and Development in Education* 16, 2 (Winter 1983): 45-52.

Chapter 8.
Curriculum From a Global Perspective

ULF P. LUNDGREN

Today's international scene calls for the development of a broader view of the scope and aim of education as a science. Educational research has been an active part of the fragmentation of education during this century. If intellectuals have a responsibility it is to unify what is fragmented and to provide a solid base for the critical understanding of changes. Science does not control these changes but can, by the power of knowledge, map them out. In that sense curriculum in a global perspective is a moral creed for scientific pedagogical enquiry. What is presented here represents the outline of a method for such an enquiry.

The Concept of Curriculum

The quantitative growth of educational research, in the western capitalist world, especially since World War II, was intimately related to the general expansion of public education. As educational science became a part of a larger social reform movement, educational knowledge was increasingly used for social engineering. Educational science thus came to be regarded not only as a basis for the rational improvement of teaching, but a basis for social planning as well. Educational research shifted from its classical orientation—

Ulf P. Lundgren is Professor, Stockholm Institute of Education, Stockholm, Sweden.

the study of education as a social institution—to an orientation toward knowledge production that was pragmatic in nature. Empirical research came to dominate the science of education.

In the 1960s and the early 70s the signs of a shift away from this post-WW II orientation became apparent. In their book *Ideology and Power*, Karabel and Halsey[1] describe the background for this shift in the direction of educational research in the United Kingdom. They note the growing interest in classical studies in education as well as an increased interest in the sociology of education. This shift was also noted in the 71st Yearbook of the National Study of Education, *Philosophical Re-directions of Educational Research*. In the preface, L. G. Thomas writes:

> In recent years educational philosophers have been turning to quite different problems and hence offering a quite different contribution to educational thought. Instead of building prescriptive theories, they have been analyzing the meaning, of educational concepts.[2]

A common problem dealt with in most of the contributions to this book is the need for conceptual stringency in the language used by researchers. Several authors deal with the fact that key concepts in educational science lack definitional rigor. Or to use the words of Komisar:

> In education, then, it is not the language that is distinct and special but rather its users. The language of education is the common language of daily affairs as used by a specific identifiable group of persons in the conduct of a distinct set of tasks.[3]

The validity of Komisar's remark can be illustrated by comparing the different meanings given to the word "curriculum" by educational researchers.

Although curriculum can be regarded as one of the key concepts in educational research,[4] it has been used quite differently by various researchers, and, in many instances, what is meant by the term is quite obscure. Dottrens[5] notes that the term curriculum in the early part of this century seems to have meant a document showing a detailed plan for a school year. Today the term "syllabus" conveys this meaning, which is also the meaning of the French term "Plan d'études," the German term "Lehrplan," and the Swedish term "Läroplan." In Swedish there is, to take one example, no term for the general concept of curriculum. In Swedish educational research the term "Läroplan" is used to cover the specific meaning, "syllabus"—namely a document, decided upon by the parliament, concerning the goals of school subjects, number of lessons per grade, and suggestions concerning the method of instruction—*and* the more general meaning of curriculum as a structured series of learning outcomes.[6] The meaning of curriculum is hence difficult to comprehend even for the educational researchers whose work is supposed to aid in the construction of curriculum theories.

The traditional and classical European school curriculum was organized within the seven liberal arts (*Trivium* and *Quadrivium*). These arts became a scholastic canon whose impact is still felt in western curriculum thinking. The liberal arts were considered to be the vehicle for the education of free men (in contrast to slaves). It was during the Middle Ages that the selection of content within the seven liberal arts came from a population of texts, the mastering of which became codified as the medium by which the mind was to be liberated and the character disciplined. Over time this changed, and the justification for the study of specific texts became the need of exemplary studies. These texts reflected the classical world ideas, and the curriculum for classical study was built on "the Golden Age concept." The goal of education, then, was to reproduce the intellectual world of the lost "Golden Ages" or the *enkyklos paidea*: the core of knowledge for all educated and scholared. The educational term for the seven liberal arts was, however, not curriculum. During the Middle Ages the terms *studium* or *ordo* and, later, *ratio, formula,* and *institution* dominated. During the 16th and 17th centuries the term *curriculum* was employed to indicate the time process; the repeatable; the coming back every year. During the Enlightenment, new terms, such as "Lehrplan" in Germany,[7] replaced the term *curriculum*. The term survived, however, in the Anglo-Saxon countries and is now reappearing in German curriculum literature.[8] In Sweden the term curriculum is still not used.

What then would constitute a rigorous definition of curriculum? As a first approximation I use the following definition: a curriculum is a *text* for pedagogy. It codifies the basic meaning of the educational process in question, the selection and organization of what is taught, and the methods for instruction. That definition conveys the sense of one given by Johnson,[9] but enlarges the scope by including the process of selection. In doing that we follow the German literature.[10] It is important to keep in mind that this definition of curriculum only has meaning and power as part of a larger conceptual framework. Therefore, in order to clarify my definition of curriculum, I will sketch out the basis for understanding state-arranged schooling in general. From within this general perspective I will identify basic problems and questions in curriculum construction and processing. Thus a global perspective is a specific theoretical perspective that can serve as a framework for identifying basic problems of schooling.

Since educational science lacks the necessary language and concepts by which basic pedagogical problems can be scientifically identified and interpreted, the terms used in educational science have a specific conceptual meaning *only* within a given conceptual frame of reference and by virtue of a specific set of relations to reality. It follows, therefore, that a global theoretical framework for curriculum can only emerge from an analysis of education as an institution and an analysis of how this institution is constituted within society.

Basically, all education is preserving or, to allude to Dewey's words in *Democracy and Education*,[11] education is the instrument for the social control of life. It is by the processes we call upbringing and education (that is, pedagogy in its most elaborated meaning) that a culture is preserved, reproduced, and renewed. In the upbringing and education of each new generation, language, the knowledge and the skills necessary for the production of goods, and the moral order of society are reproduced. Durkheim writes:

> Every society sets up certain ideals of man, of what he should be, as much from the intellectual point of view as the physical and moral. The ideal is, in some degree, the same for all members of society; but also it becomes differential beyond a certain point, according to the specific groupings that every society contains in its structure. It is the ideal, which is both integral and diverse, that is the focus of education.[12]

The ideal Durkheim describes is a *historical* product explainable in relation to changes in modes of production and changes in social organization and culture. Simply stated, social ideals must be understood in terms of the particular historical context from which they emerged.

Social *production* involves the transformation of the natural world into objects and social necessities as well as the production of symbols and the social conditions necessary to enable production to continue. The goals, content, and structure of social *reproduction* reflect the modes of social *production*, the *historical conditions* that have formed the modes of production, and the *production structure*.

Since cultural and social reproduction assumes its form in pedagogic processes, the nature of these pedagogical processes is necessarily a function of the sociocultural context in which they are constituted. In order to explain the nature of social reproduction it is useful to examine the division of pedagogic responsibility in society. It may be helpful to make a distinction between two agencies of social reproduction: (1) the primary social group and (2) the state (the term state confined to its Weberian connotation; institutions in society that have the legitimate right to use violence).

In a society characterized by a limited social division of labor, and having a homogeneous culture—for example, a stable agriculture society—the education of the child in the primary social group is sufficient to guarantee the reproduction of the knowledge and skills necessary for production. It can even be argued that in such a society there exist few if no concepts that are educational in nature. The selection of content for education and for upbringing is given by the context. In other words, *education is embedded in the social context*. The selection and organization of content is given by the social life itself. There is no need for an educational language and even the transmission of knowledge can be done with relatively few symbols. In such societies learning is, to use Dewey's characterization of the nature of learning and education, "the organic connection between education and personal experience."[13] Children learn, for example, by imitating adults. Through imitation they learn to identify with the culture and its forms of management of the world about them.[14] Socialization is based on children's *direct* relationship to the world around them. The value and meaning of work is learned *at the same time* as the knowledge and skills necessary for work. The recreation of knowledge and skills required for production is intimately and indissolubly interwoven with the recreation of the cultural values and ideas that are essential for the moral order. Thus the ideal of education is a consensus within the group responsible for education. The responsibility of the state (if we can talk meaningfully of a state in such a society) is limited to the needs of the state itself; that is, the need for qualified manpower to carry out its military, judicial and administrative functions. Using Durkheim's terms we can talk about such a society as being characterized by *mechanical solidarity*.

Ideas about public education in Europe are a part of European religious tradition. With the reformations of the church, religious education became public education. The emergence of new national states, exemplified by the French and the American Revolutions, created the need for the public education of citizens—a public education motivated by national constitutions. "I know no safe depository of the ultimate powers of society but the people themselves," wrote Thomas Jefferson, "and if we think them not enlightened enough to exercise their control with a wholesome discretion, the remedy is not to take it from them, but to inform their discretion by education."[15] Jefferson argued for public education in order to guarantee the new Republic. These ideas about public education must also be understood in relation not only to new conceptions of the relation between state and society, but also in relation to basic societal changes. The establishment of compulsory public education, for example, was in part a consequence of basic changes in structure of production of western society.

The rationalization of agriculture in the 18th and 19th centuries, for example, changed the modes of production in the western world. The development of new energy forms laid the ground work for industrialization. Basic changes in capital structure signified the emergence of a new economic structure. A new division of labor increased the differentiation within western societies. Urbanization was partly a consequence of the effects of the agricultural rationalization and partly a consequence of an increasing proletarianization of the workers of the soil. This process supported accelerated industrialization by creating a pool of labor for industrial expansion.

The composition of the bourgeois strata was also changed by the increasing industrialization.[16] These social changes meant a stratification of the traditional bourgeois into new groups, which were based on educational qualifications in addition to the possession of movable capital. A new "middling class" was formed that put new demands on the state, which included demands for education.

This web of changes of the material base and superstructure of western society cannot be explained in chains of cause and effect. They are changes produced by human work and activity, both physical and mental. Describing these changes in terms of their educational significance, we see them as breaking the *organic relationship* between social production and social reproduction.

The Birth of Compulsory School Curriculum

Two points from the preceding discussion have to be repeated. First, in notes about the genesis of the term curriculum, I pointed out that the classical curriculum initially centered around the education of free men, and was later trapped in a tradition of mastering certain texts. Second, education in a society with a limited division of labor, the educational problems of the selection, and the organization of content for pedagogy was simply a part of the social context of production. These two points are important in the discussion to come.

During the 1830s and 1840s, laws were passed concerning compulsory education in most countries in Europe. The state assumed a responsibility (education) that had previously been the responsibility of primary social groups and tried to transmit a moral picture to the citizens that was, to use Durkheim's word, integral.

It is when the processes of production and reproduction are separated and fragmented that the concept of curriculum becomes a social necessity. When we are able to identify the *two* basic contexts in a society (production *and* reproduction), what should be learned, how it should be organized, and how the instruction is to be formed are no longer embedded *in* the production context. Instead they become abstract problems that have to be conceptualized separate from the production process. The knowledge and skills to be learned are no longer given by the immediate context; rather, they have to be abstracted out of that context and delivered in a *text*. In compulsory mass public education there is no context for education that *by itself* organizes what is worth knowing. A *selection* has to be made, this selection has to be organized, and forms for instruction have to be developed. More concretely: if learning how to use the plough is in the context of ploughing and the knowledge and skills are acquired in the real context of ploughing, then the activity itself will determine the selection of content, organization of content, and methods of transmission. In an educational institution the plough is replaced by a picture, and the transmission of knowledge about the plough must be done by language. It becomes important to name the parts of the plough, to be able to describe the process of ploughing, to learn via abstract thinking what practical experience could teach. In other words, the plough becomes abstraction. Or in still other words, the plough is *"decontextualized."*

The point is that when production and reproduction processes in a society are inextricably interwoven, the problems of social reproduction are very intimately related to the problems of social production. The child learns the knowledge and skills necessary for production by participating in the production processes. There is no need for a special language for education; there is no need for thinking in terms of objectives, goals, or methods for teaching. The problem of learning is a part of production, and evaluation is the working process itself. A slow learner means slower production. When production and reproduction processes are separated from each other a *representation problem* arises; that is, the problem is how to *represent* production processes so they can be reproduced. The representation problem is the object of educational discourse, and its specific solution is the curriculum. Thus the concept of curriculum in the context of compulsory public education addresses *the transformation of a contextualized pedagogy to a decontextualized pedagogy.*

A Method of Enquiry

Let us return to the discussion about the lack of specificity in the language of education as a science. If we accept the statement that education as a science has few concepts that are well defined, one explanation is that educational research is only to a small degree built on a basic knowledge of the reality to be studied. Since educational research has become (1) linked to social/education change, and (2) instrumental in its aims, the criteria for knowledge production in education have been contextually bound to the specific sort of education the research was supposed to serve. These statements follow from the observation that the terms used in educational research more often reflect a specific educational system, and thereby a specific culture, than a fundamental scientific and theoretical tradition. To illustrate the same point in a more specific way, Walker argues that the research tradition "does not stem from any intrinsic qualities of behaviour, but rather is derived from the moral order of American culture."[17] If a key concept in a science is arbitrarily used, that is, as Komisar pointed out, it is specific only by virtue of the fact that its user has conducted a distinct set of tasks, then this concept is a function of the context in which the users dwell. The result is that the research will produce theories that are arbitrary and bound to time and context.

According to Tornebohn, scientific enquiry and research is:

> ... sequences of complexes composed by knowledge, problems, and instruments ... It will be assumed that research is concerned with a part of the real world. Knowledge may then be described as an authorized map over the territory.[18]

The need then is to develop a scientific perspective that *both* defines the territory and assigns value to the map. If we accept that the territory of education is an artifact and that educational phenomena are human-made and therefore historically constituted,

> Whatever regularities researchers are to find in educational phenomena will have been determined by human beings in a social context. Normative judgements (rules, policies, value judgements, ideals which govern action) condition greatly the phenomena to be studied. Change a belief system and the content of research reports will be different.[19]

These explanations help illustrate the necessity of developing a scientific perspective *within which* key concepts have clear meaning, that is, a perspective concerning the basic phenomena of education. It is a perspective I have chosen to call a global perspective, which requires that the birth of schooling as a context for reproduction has to be conceptualized. Schooling—the creation of a specific human activity for the socialization of children, separated from basic social production—has to be conceptualized, so that key educational concepts can be given precise meaning. In other words, the conceptualization of schooling will make us able to conceptualize the entire field of education.

The basic problems that Dewey and Durkheim dealt with were the educational consequences of a modern society in which schooling replaced the education and upbringing in homes. Their work concerned the consequences of a differentiated society in which the production processes and the reproduction processes were separated from each other. Dewey's work concerned how to break the consequential abstraction process in schooling. How to make, via public education, a differentiated and therefore relatively invisible society more visible; how to create an organic link between education and personal experience; or, in other words, how to *recontextualize* education. Durkheim saw the same social differentiation as the basic shaping process of modern society and modern culture. This process, according to Durkheim, resulted in the breaking down of a mechanical solidarity and created the problem of how to shape a new organic solidarity. In this context, modern society, the moral order had to be guaranteed by the state. Modern public schooling was, then, created to transmit a moral order, which, because of social differentiation and the increasing division of labor, could not be secured *within* the processes of production.

The conceptual framework being constructed here contains two pairs of concepts that are dialectically related to each other. One pair is production/reproduction. The other pair is state/society. Taking this paradigm as a structure in analyzing the historical development of society, I have utilized the concepts of *pedagogical context* and *pedagogical text*. When production and reproduction processes are separated, two pedagogic *contexts* are created: (1) the context of *society*, in which education is conducted in the primary social group and related to the social production, and (2) context of *schools*, in which education is arranged by the state and in which education is conducted in schools. Given this separation of social production and reproduction and the creation of a specific context for reproduction (schools), education becomes abstract, decontextualized, and processed by and through *texts*. Education develops as a special field of discourse. A language about education is formed; text traditions are established. Ideas about the methods of transmission are formed. The curriculum field within mass education is made possible.

This paradigm is not a theory in a restrictive sense. It is a scientific perspective within which key concepts can be defined and within which specific theories can be formed by empirical studies. It is a perspective that delivers a specific language that makes it possible to compare and use various specific theories related to time and context-bound educational phenomena. It is a method of enquiry in that it gives a theoretical frame of reference for questioning specific phenomena.

Curriculum and Schooling

In sketching this perspective we relied on a series of approximations. The purpose was to illuminate the conditions under which the state has intervened in social reproduction.

One such approximation was the statement that the separation of production processes from reproduction processes called for new forms of social
integration. Industrialization, the rationalization of farming, migration, and
new political ideas and theories changed the social structure of the western
world during the 19th century. Sweden is an example of how farming was
rationalized. Laws were passed in the late 18th century and early 19th century
requiring that farm properties be divided in a new way. Formerly, the village
was the social center, and one farm could, through heritage, have small parcels
of land distributed in many places. This demanded cooperation in the village
and farmers were thus dependent on each other. The new laws divided
properties so that farmhouses were moved out to the properties and the
village structure was destroyed. Farming became more efficient and the population grew, but children were not allowed to divide the property. The
younger children had to find work outside the farm. In this way a proletariat
was formed that later provided the labor force for expanding industry. From
a reproduction point of view, established patterns broke down. Parents lived
far away from their children who had to raise their own children in a new
social context, which in turn changed the nature of social reproduction.

The breakdown of the social structure with the rationalization of farming
and industrialization occasioned new social problems and social turbulence.
The working class was formed and the bourgeois classes were divided into
new strata. In 1848 there were revolutions in most of the capitals of Europe.
In England social contradictions had led to the People's Charter (1838). The
Communist Manifesto published in 1848 ends with: "Let the ruling classes
tremble at a Communistic revolution. The proletarians have nothing to lose
but their chains. They have a world to win. Working men of all countries,
Unite!" This was an expression of internationalism that threatened national
states.

Internationalism and attacks on the existing social order were met with
both force and social plans. The passage of compulsory education laws is an
example of a social plan. The aims of the curriculums for this new mass
education were to train the citizens in their duties. The curriculums for the
compulsory schools became, then, curriculums built on a moral code. The
purpose of pedagogical texts was to transmit a basic moral order. Earlier I
described the classical curriculum as built on a specific text-tradition. It was
a specific set of texts that were to be reproduced. The concept of a well-
educated man was constructed first on the ideal of a liberated man mastering
the world about him by an education that was an odyssey through the existing
and the lost world. Later this odyssey became a piloted tour—the word
curriculum stood for the repeatable, the coming back, the scheduled. This

was a very specific meaning of curriculum, in which the curriculum was bound to an organized set of *texts*.

I have defined curriculum as the basic meaning of what is to be learned, a meaning that governs the selection of content, the organization of content, and the ideas of instruction. I have also, within this general definition, discussed the birth of curriculum in mass education by explaining the necessity of mass education and schooling as a consequence of basic changes in society, related to division of labor. I have also stated that in the first phase of mass education, the basic code—the basic meaning of the curriculum governing the selection, organization, and ideals of instruction—was a moral one. By the term *curriculum code* I mean a set of principles that guide the selection and organization of content and form the ideals and practice of instruction.[20]

To say that curriculum becomes a necessity when schooling is established is *not* to say that the curriculum has to take the form of a document. It can as well be a shared view on what is important to reproduce, or a consensus. It *is* to say, however, that the educational processes will have a specific meaning, which is the transmission of a curriculum code.

With the introduction of modern languages and modern natural sciences, the classical curriculum code partially disappeared, and was combined with a more *realistic* curriculum code. After the French Revolution, natural science as a part of the curriculum became a reality. In the U.S. Samuel Smith advocated a realistic curriculum responsive to modern American society. The study of natural sciences had come to have a practical value. New disciplines like mechanics, geography, natural history, and linear drawing were introduced. The methods of instruction changed. Laboratories were used. The microscope was introduced into education as well as audiovisual material (such as model ships and model gardens). This shift announced a new relationship between state and society. The changes in the bourgeois strata had put demands on the state to assume a responsibility for a specific type of education (realistic) in addition to the education needed for the management of the state apparatus itself.

Returning to the two pairs of concepts in the paradigm, we can see how the destruction of the organic relation between production and reproduction appeared, on the one hand, as the educational problems of providing necessary new qualifications as well as education for a new type of "free men," *and*, on the other hand, appeared as a reproduction failure that called for a new moral education of the masses. The result is state intervention in social reproduction. The resulting state-organized educational system designed to respond to these problems was built on two pillars. The first pillar was a curriculum that developed from a long text tradition, built on elements from classical curriculum thinking, with new principles into which more pragmatic elements had been introduced. The second pillar is a school system designed to provide moral training, that is, training for citizenship.

The Modern Curriculum—The Reconstruction of the Invisible Community

With the increased separation of production processes from reproduction processes, demands on public education were more and more related to the lost link between production and reproduction. That is, public schools were expected to integrate the reproduction of knowledge and skills not only with the dominant moral order, but also to integrate them with the modes of production and thereby provide the *qualifications* needed for production. It was, however, not only qualifications in a strict sense that were needed. With the increasing differentiation within society and the increasing division of labor, society in itself became for the single citizen more and more invisible. Education, for which the state was now responsible, had to intervene to recreate for the citizen a picture of lost relations. In their essay, *"The Invisible and Lost Community of Work and Education,"* Eleanor and Walter Feinberg write:

> It is not so much the case that the moral justification of work is new. Plato's Republic was, at the very least, an attempt to justify work on moral ground. What is new is the fact that for many people the context of this justification is an abstract one, one that is not easily reinforced by the direct effect that their work has on the lives of other people . . . The community which we serve is an abstract one, and therefore the moral justification which allows us to continue in our work is indeed best represented by a picture, by a copy of reality that is in fact too large for us to experience. Where a community is present, then we can take it for granted, and concern ourselves with workmanship. Where it is not present, we must create it in our hand and must worry about making a contribution.[21]

The successive fragmentations of production and reproduction produced a new legitimation for education. Schools were to educate a new type of citizen. These citizens would (1) understand their role in a new and democratic society, (2) be able to cope with abstract knowledge about reality, and (3) accept work dependent on mental capacity and thereby on education. In perhaps one of his most influential works, *The School and Society*, Dewey writes:

> One can hardly believe there has been a revolution in all history so rapid, so extensive, so complete (p. 35) . . . Back of the factory systems lies the household and neighborhood system. Those of us who are here today need go back only

one, two or at most three generations, to find a time when the household was practically the center in which were carried on, or about which were clustered, all the typical forms of industry (p. 36) . . . At present, concentration of industry and division of labor have practically eliminated household and neighborhood occupations—at least for the educational purpose.[22]

The solution to come was a pedagogy in which the curriculum was organized around the individual. Even the very definition of curriculum became an individual learning sequence, as in the 1969 edition of *Encyclopedia of Educational Research*, in which Kearney and Cook define curriculum as ". . . all experiences a learner has under the guidance of the school."[23] We can describe this definition of curriculum as being structured around a *rational* curriculum code; that is, the curriculum should be selected in relation to the knowledge and skills needed. The organization was to follow the cognitive development of the child with the methods of instruction being built on the needs of the child. Given this definition, not only was the past to be reproduced, but the future was to be created as well.

The central place given to individuals and their potential by the rational curriculum code meant that the school had to be organized to give each individual the same possibility, and this meant that the two streams and traditions of schooling (the moral and classical/realistic) had to be unified. The legitimacy of such a curriculum and organization for schooling was that it provided equal opportunity.

During this century the nature of schooling has been debated and affected by the concepts of school differentiation and discipline-oriented education versus comprehensive schools and child-centered education, for example. However, irrespective of these debates, the main point was one made by Dewey: education in modern society will by necessity be more abstract and text-bound. Dewey essentially attempted to recontextualize education, to build up a new context for education instead of restoring the lost natural context (that of household and neighborhood work). To some extent the progressivistic ideas of Dewey became rhetoric. The legitimacy of modern curriculum lay in the knowledge and skills it provided that were supposed to guarantee a value on the labor market.

A basic paradox was therefore built into education: state-arranged education had to, on one hand, adjust to production and the division of labor and, on the other hand, create equal chances independent of society. In other words the paradox is an educational system that reproduces the basic structure of society and thereby reflects the social structure of that society, and at the same time is independent of that society. To return to Dewey,

> If we go back a few centuries we find a practical monopoly of learning. The term *possession* of learning was, indeed, a happy one. Learning was a class matter. This was a necessary result of social conditions. There were not in existence any means by which the multitude could possibly have access to intellectual resources. These were stored up and hidden away in manuscripts.[24]

But in the modern society this has changed.

> The result has been an intellectual revolution. Learning has been put into circulation. While there still is, and probably always will be, a particular class having the special business of inquiry in hand, a distinctively learned class is henceforth out of the question. It is anachronism. Knowledge is no longer an immobile solid; it has been liquified. It is actively moving in all currents of society itself.[25]

To some extent this anachronism, if it is an anachronism, is still there. What Dewey believed in was the rapid break of traditions and the victory of a "rational society." But in modern industrialized and capitalistic societies any curriculum for public education must be built on a selection and organization of what is to be learned. Because modern society is differentiated and socially stratified, and social organization illustrates that social position and thus the power and control of classes, groups, and individuals is related to the modes of production, the selection and organization of what is to be learned in school (how the content and methods of teaching are classified and framed) is a question of how the social stratification is reproduced. It focuses on where the power and control in society are located, and how this power and control are filtered by the traditions of education and channeled by the state. It is in explaining this dynamic relationship between power and control and its social base that Bernstein[26] has made his very important scientific contributions. The theory developed by Bernstein gives us a powerful instrument to answer basic questions of curriculum theory; how a specific pedagogy is constituted and legitimated; how a specific social stratification is reproduced by a specific curriculum.

The Curriculum Crisis

Crisis means turning point. In some sense we can see a crisis in modern curriculum. The expansion of education seems to have reached a turning point. In the western world new priorities have emerged in the public sector and the limits of state intervention in education seem to have been reached. A new space for private education seems to have opened up. The legitimacy of education in relation to the life of work and the labor market also seems to have reached a turning point. The youth unemployment problem seems unsolvable in the near future. The expansion of the labor market is reaching a turning point because of electronic rationalization.

We can see the ideological consequences of these processes in the educational debate of the last three decades. Three types of curriculum solutions have been advocated. One is the traditional "regression," the call for what has been lost, the days when there was a link between education and the world of work; back to basics and back to the "old" traditional science and discipline-oriented curriculum. The second is the renewal of the curriculum with the aid of new technology; data knowledge, computer knowledge, and programming as essential cores of the curriculum. The third is the adaption and accepting of conditions; curriculums for the unemployed; "schooling is no longer question of getting work but a question of finding a mode of living." Of course, none of these solutions is in any sense a solution of the basic problem of how to create a meaningful link between production and reproduction processes in society.

The crisis is here. Leaving the normative-political questions of how to form solutions and focusing on the scientific questions about how to deal with and explain modern education, I believe the answers should be sought in the analyses of the basic dialectic relations between production-reproduction processes and state-society relations.

If the modern curriculum is in a crisis as a consequence of changes in the modes and conditions of production *for which there is no corresponding process of reproduction*, as well because changes in the material and ideological relations between state and society, we can identify profound questions to be dealt with in analyzing state-arranged education in capitalistic societies with a high level of industrialization. These questions have to be formed in relation to the conditions existing in these societies, although their answers and the resulting theories will be specific to these conditions. The curriculum crisis in modern capitalistic societies has an impact on other societies as well. The educational systems in the communist world, for example, reflect the educational system in the capitalist world in several aspects. The technology linked to the military and industry and to space programs have partly taken over the development of technology to be adapted for industrial production. In other words, technical development is more and more governed by military demands. Thus the new technology and new knowledge implemented in curriculums is determined in a broad sense by the world political situation. In that respect the educational systems in capitalistic and communist countries are interdependent. But this interdependence can only be seen and explained by theories that build on the study of how new knowledge and technology is produced and how it is built into curriculums.

Another type of interdependence exists between the developed and the developing countries of the world. In developing countries, state-arranged education has to cope with implementing curriculums for a society that is in rapid change. In many of these societies there is still an organic link between the production and reproduction processes. This means that the long-term historical development of western schooling with its continuous adjustment to changes in the relations between production and reproduction over hundreds of years is forced into a context in which the relations between production and reproduction is quite different. In developing countries traditional society lives side by side with modern industrialized society. The conflicts over the reproduction of values, skills, and knowledges from these different parts of society can be violent, which invites violence by the state. At the same time, the state apparatus often not only depends on its own production but on international contributions and loans as well. This means that legitimacy of the educational system is established not only in terms of the developing society, but in terms of developed countries. Thus, while the state apparatus has power in relation to its own society, it may be powerless in relation to other nations and economic systems. The crisis of the modern educational system is a fundamental fact of life for developing countries.

Curriculum in a Global Perspective

To close the circle, I have outlined the contours of a paradigm of thinking—a method of enquiry. The paradigm builds on the dialectic relationship between social production and social reproduction *and* state and society. In order to understand education as a social institution, we have to understand the structural development of western societies. This development can be seen as qualitative steps of development. The separation of reproduction from production resulted in the social phenomena of schooling. The qualitative changes in the relation between state and society has called for an increasing intervention by the state in education. The constitution of specific contexts for reproduction (schools) means that learning to cope with culture and the world of work is through abstract thinking and that teaching is processed by texts. The development of educational institutions has created the phenomena of the curriculum.

With the aid of the concepts used I have tried to point out what I have called the crisis of modern curriculum. I have done that in some brief notes containing reflections over interdependence among educational systems in capitalistic, communistic, and developing countries. With that, I return to the commonsense meaning of the title of this chapter.

Notes

[1]J. Karabel and A. H. Halsey, *Power and Ideology in Education* (New York: Oxford University Press, 1978).

[2]L. G. Thomas, ed., *Philosophical Redirections of Educational Research*, 71st yearbook of the National Society for the Study of Education (Chicago: University of Chicago Press, 1972), p. 1.

[3]B. P. Komisar, "Language of Education," 1971, p. 328.

[4]D. Kallos and U. P. Lundgren, *Curriculum as a Pedagogical Problem* (Lund: Liber, 1979).

[5]R. Dottrens, *The Primary School Curriculum* (Paris: UNESCO, Monographs on Education II, 1962).

[6]M. Johnson, Jr., "Definitions and Models in Curriculum Theory," *International Review of Education* 19 (1967): 187-194.

[7]H. Blankertz, *Theorien und Modelle der Didaktik* (Munchen: Juventa Verlag, 1980).

[8]K. Frey and others, *Curriculum Handbook* (Munchen: R. Piper Verlag, 1975).

[9]Johnson, ibid.

[10]Blankertz, ibid.; U. P. Lundgren, *Att organisera omvärlden. En introduktion till läroplansteori* (To Organize the World About Us. In Introduction to Curriculum Theory) (Stockholm: Liber, 1979); U. P. Lundgren, *Between Hope and Happening*. Text and Context in Curriculum Development (Geelong: Deakin University Press, 1983).

[11]J. Dewey, *Democracy and Education* (New York: The Macmillan Co., 1916).

[12]E. Durkheim, *Education and Sociologie*. Translated in English in A. Giddens, *Emilie Durkheim, Selected Writings* (London: Cambridge University Press, 1972), p. 203.

[13]J. Dewey, *Experience and Education* (New York: The Macmillan Co., 1938), p. 12.

[14]J. Hart, *A Social Interpretation of Education* (New York: Henry Holt and Company, 1929).

[15]G. G. Lee, *Crusade Against Ignorance. Thomas Jefferson on Education* (New York: Columbia University, Teachers College Press, 1961).

[16]R. S. Neale, *Class and Ideology in the Nineteenth Century* (London: Sage Publication, 1972).

[17]R. Walker, "General Problems That Arise When Interaction Analysis is Used to Assess the Impact of Educational Innovation," *Classroom Interaction Newsletter* 7 (1972): 38-49.

[18]H. Tornebohm, *Reflections in Scientific Research* (Göteborg: Institute for the Theory of Science, 1971).

[19]D. D. Gowin, "Is Educational Research Distinctive?" (1972).

[20]Lundren, 1979; Lundgren, 1983.

[21]E. Feinberg and W. Feinberg, *The Invisible and Lost Community of Work and Education*, Reports on Education and Psychology No. 1 (Stockholm: Stockholm Institute of Education, 1979).

[22]M. S. Dworkin, *Dewey on Education*, Classics on Education No. 3 (New York: Teachers College Press, 1959).

[23]N. C. Kearney and W. W. Cook, "Curriculum," *Business Review* XXXVI (1958): 23-30.

[24]J. Dewey, *The School and Society* (Chicago: University of Chicago Press, 1899), from Dworkin, op. cit., p. 46.

[25]Ibid., pp. 46-47.

[26]B. Bernstein, *Class, Codes and Control. Vol. 3: Towards a Theory of Transmissions* (London: Routledge & Kegan Paul, 1977); B. Bernstein, *Codes, Modalities and the Process of Cultural Reproduction: A Model*, Pedagogical Bulletin No. 7 (Lund: University of Lund, 1980).

ASCD Board of Directors

Executive Council
1984-85

President: Phil C. Robinson, Principal, Clarence B. Sabbath School, River Rouge, Michigan

President-Elect: Carolyn Sue Hughes, Principal, Ludlow School, Shaker Heights, Ohio

Immediate Past-President: Lawrence S. Finkel, Executive Director, Institute for Curriculum Development, Dobbs Ferry, New York; Graduate School, College of New Rochelle, New Rochelle, New York

Patricia C. Conran, Superintendent, Benjamin School District #5, West Chicago, Illinois

Sidney H. Estes, Assistant Superintendent, Atlanta Public Schools, Atlanta, Georgia

Robert C. Hanes, Deputy Superintendent of Schools, Charlotte/Mecklenburg Schools, Charlotte, North Carolina

Francis P. Hunkins, Professor of Education, University of Washington, Seattle

Anna Jolivet, Director of Planning Services, Tucson Unified School District, Tucson, Arizona

Luther L. Kiser, Assistant Superintendent of Curriculum and Instruction, Ames Community School District, Ames, Iowa

Marcia Knoll, Principal, Public School 220, Queens, Forest Hills, New York

Elizabeth R. Lane, Principal, Mount Pisgah Elementary School, Memphis, Tennessee

Nelson Quinby, Director of Secondary Education, Joel Barlow High School, West Redding, Connecticut

Robert L. Sigmon, Director of Elementary Education, Richmond City Schools, Richmond, Virginia

Board Members Elected at Large

(Listed alphabetically; the year in parentheses indicates the end of the term of office.)

Richard Babb, City of Auburn Public Schools, Auburn, Maine (1986)

Roger Bennett, University of Wisconsin, Oshkosh, Wisconsin (1987)

Doris Brown, University of Missouri, St. Louis, Missouri (1987)

Donna Jean Carter, Robbinsdale Area Independent School District #281, Minneapolis, Minnesota (1988)

Gene Raymond Carter, Norfolk Public Schools, Norfolk, Virginia (1985)

Geneva Gay, Purdue University, West Lafayette, Indiana (1987)

Delores Greene, Richmond Public Schools, Richmond, Virginia (1988)

Elaine McNally Jarchow, Iowa State University, Ames, Iowa (1985)

Lois Harrison-Jones, Richmond City Schools, Richmond, Virginia (1986)

Jessie Kobayashi, Berryessa Unified School District, San Jose, California (1986)

Richard Kunkel, National Council for Accreditation of Teacher Education, Washington, D.C. (1988)

Marian Leibowitz, Teaneck Board of Education, Teaneck, New Jersey (1986)

Betty Livengood, Mineral County Schools, Keyser, West Virginia (1985)
E. Gaye McGovern, East Palestine City School District, East Palestine, Ohio (1985)
Arthur D. Roberts, University of Connecticut, Storrs, Connecticut (1987)
Ann Converse Shelly, Bethany College, Bethany, West Virginia (1986)
Arthur Steller, Mercer County Public Schools, Princeton, West Virginia (1987)
Laurel Tanner, Temple University, Philadelphia, Pennsylvania (1985)
Lois Fair Wilson, Redlands, California (1988)
Claire Yoshida, Office of Instructional Services, Honolulu, Hawaii (1988)

Unit Representatives to the Board of Directors

(Each unit's president is listed first.)

Alabama: Milly Cowles, University of Alabama, Birmingham; James Condra,
    University of Alabama, Gadsden; Mabel Robinson, University of Alabama,
    Birmingham
Alaska: Emma Walton, Anchorage School District, Anchorage; Denice Clyne, Sand
    Lake School, Anchorage
Arizona: Susan Masek, Craycroft Elementary School, Tucson; Ellie Sbragia, Arizona
    Center for Law Related Education, Phoenix; Darleen Videen, Pima County
    Schools, Tucson
Arkansas: David Robinson, Sheridan Public Schools, Sheridan; Philip Besonen,
    University of Arkansas, Fayetteville
California: Doris Prince, Santa Clara County Schools, San Jose; Walter Klas, Alameda
    Unified School District, Alameda; Nancy Murray Comstock, Kern County
    Schools, Bakersfield; Bill James, Paso Robles Joint Union HSD, Paso Robles; Jean
    Dudley Upton, Madera Unified School District, Chowchilla; Bob Guerts, Sonoma
    Valley Unified School District, Santa Rosa; David Philips, Encinatas Union,
    Encinatas; Shareen Young, Santa Clara County Office of Education, San Jose
Colorado: Mel Preusser, Douglas County School District, Castle Rock; Donna
    Brennen, Cherry Creek School District, Englewood; Cile Chavez, Littleton Public
    Schools, Littleton
Connecticut: Arthur Roberts, University of Connecticut, Storrs; Thomas Jokubaitis,
    Wolcott Public Schools, Wolcott; Bernard Goffin, Monroe Public Schools,
    Monroe
Delaware: Frank P. Jelich, Delaware Department of Public Instruction, Dover;
    Melville Warren, Capital School District, Dover
District of Columbia: Vivian Archer, Savoy Administrative Unit, Washington, D.C.;
    Roberta Walker, Chapter One Program, Washington, D.C.
Florida: Jean Marani, Department of Education, Tallahassee; Eileen Duval, Buckhorn
    Elementary School, Valrico; Hilda Wiles, Littlewood Elementary School,
    Gainesville; Mary Jo Sisson, Okaloosa County School District, Fort Walton Beach
Georgia: Gerard F. Lentini, West Georgia College, Carrollton; Priscilla Doster,
    Monroe City Schools, Forsyth; Scott Bradshaw, Georgia Department of
    Education, Atlanta
Hawaii: Mary M. Logasa, Lanikai School, Kailua; Virgie Chattergy, University of
    Hawaii, Honolulu

Idaho: Gary Doramus, Woodrow Wilson Elementary, Caldwell; David Carroll, Boise
    Public Schools, Boise
Illinois: John W. Fletcher, Park Ridge School District, Park Ridge; Rodney M. Borstad,
    North Illinois University, DeKalb; Patricia C. Conran, Benjamin School District
    #5, West Chicago; Al Cohen, Wilmot Junior High School, Deerfield; Richard
    Hanke, Thomas Junior High School, Arlington Heights; Carolyn S. Kimbell,
    Downers Grove School District #58, Downers Grove; Stephanie Marshal,
    Batavia School District #101, Batavia
Indiana: Kenneth Springer, North Adams Community Schools, Decatur; Sue Pifer,
    Bartholomew Community School Corporation, Columbus; Marvin Odom,
    Carmel-Clay Schools, Carmel
Iowa: Arnold Lindaman, North Scott Community School District, Eldridge; Harold
    Lulleman, Linn Marr Community Schools, Marion; John Watson, Muscatine
    Community Schools, Muscatine
Kansas: Doug Christensen, Colby Public Schools, Colby; Jim Jarrett, Unified School
    District #315, Kansas City; Harold E. Schmidt, Unified School District #305,
    Salina
Kentucky: Joe Clark, Kentucky Education Department, Frankfort; Tom Taylor, Owen
    City High School, Owenton; Judy Minnehan, Oldham County Board of
    Education, LaGrange
Louisiana: John Alexander, Jefferson Parish School Board, Gretna; Julianna
    Boudreaux, New Orleans Public Schools, New Orleans; Kate Scully, New
    Orleans Public Schools, New Orleans
Maine: Joan Smith, Winthrop; Ralph Egers, Superintendent of Schools Office, South
    Portland; William Richards, State House Station #23, Augusta
Maryland: Evelyn Holman, Wicomico County Board of Education, Salisbury; Thelma
    Sparks (retired), Public Schools, Annapolis; James Dudley, University of
    Maryland, College Park
Massachusetts: Robert Munnelly, Reading Public Schools, Reading; Peter Farrelly,
    Wachusett Regional Schools, Holden; Morton Milesky, Longmeadow Public
    Schools, Longmeadow; Gary G. Baker, Acton Public Schools, Acton
Michigan: Ronald L. Sergeant, Kalamazoo Valley Intermediate School, Kalamazoo;
    Virginia Sorenson, West Michigan University, Kalamazoo; Jim Perry, Muskegon
    Independent School District, Muskegon; Dixie Hibner, Saline Area Schools,
    Saline; Charles King, Michigan Education Association, East Lansing
Minnesota: Joan Black, Bloomington Public Schools, Bloomington; Merrill Fellger,
    Buffalo Public Schools, Buffalo; Karen Johnson, Independent School District
    #622, North St. Paul
Mississippi: Milton Baxter, University of South Mississippi, Hattiesburg; Bobbie
    Collum, Mississippi State Department of Education, Jackson
Missouri: Jerry Elliott, Maplewood-Richmond Heights School District, Maplewood;
    Pat Rockladge, Normandy School District, St. Louis; Cameron Pulliam, Mark
    Twain Elementary School, Brentwood
Montana: Steve Henry, Billings Elementary School District, Billings; Louise Bell,
    Eastern Montana College, Billings
Nebraska: Kenneth Rippe, Elkhorn Public Schools, Elkhorn; L. James Walter,
    University of Nebraska, Lincoln; Dave Van Horn, Everett Junior High School,
    Lincoln

Nevada: Edna Hinman, Clark County School District, Las Vegas; Jerry Conner, Nevada
    Association of School Administrators, Las Vegas
New Hampshire: Larry DiCenzo, Winnisquam Middle School, Tilton; Jean Stefanik,
    Wilkins School, Amherst
New Jersey: Thomas Lubben, Janis Dismus Middle School, Englewood; Judith
    Zimmerman, Edgar Elementary School, Metuchen; Paul Braungart, Mary Roberts
    School, Moorestown; Ruth Dorney, Ironia School, Randolph; Paul Manko, Mt.
    Laurel Board of Education, Mt. Laurel
New Mexico: Jack Bobroff, Albuquerque Public Schools, Albuquerque; Bettye Coffey,
    Albuquerque Public Schools, Albuquerque
New York: Tim Melchior, Memorial Junior High School, Valley Stream; Dorothy
    Foley, State Education Department, Schenectady; Arlene Soifer, Nassau Boces,
    Carle Place; Anthony Deiulio, State University College, Fredonia; Robert Brellis,
    Idle Hour School, Oakdale; Nicholas Vitalo, Davison Avenue School, Lynbrook;
    Florence Seldin, Pittsford Central School, Pittsford; Donald Harkness, Manhasset
    Public Schools, Manhasset
North Carolina: Francine Delany, Asheville City Schools, Asheville; Hilda Olson,
    Hendersonville Public Schools, Hendersonville; Mary Jane Dillard, Jackson
    County Board of Education, Sylva
North Dakota: Richard B. Warner, Fargo South High Schoool, Fargo
Ohio: Billy Bittinger, Mad River Township Schools, Dayton; Eugene Glick, Ohio
    ASCD, Medina; Ronald Hibbard, Kenston Local School District, Chagrin Falls;
    Arthur Wohlers, Ohio State University, Columbus; Irma Lou Griggs, Lake Local
    School District, Hartville
Oklahoma: James Roberts, Lawton Public Schools, Lawton; Nelda Tebow, Educational
    Consultant, Oklahoma City; Sharon Lease, State Department of Education,
    Oklahoma City
Oregon: Zola Dunbar, Portland State University, Portland; Art Phillips (retired),
    Ashland Public Schools, Ashland; LaVae Robertson, Oak Elementary School,
    Albany
Pennsylvania: Therese Walter, General McLane School District, Edinboro; John P.
    Jarvie, Northwest Tri-County Intermediate Unit, Edinborough; Robert F. Nicely,
    Pennsylvania State University, University Park; David Campbell, Pennsylvania
    Department of Education, Harrisburg; Donald L. Wright, Montgomery County
    I.U. #23, Erdenheim
Puerto Rico: Teresa de Dios, American Military Academy, Guaynabo; Ramon M.
    Barquin, American Millitary Academy, Guaynabo
Rhode Island: Nora Walker, Public Schools, Cumberland; Guy DiBiasio, Cranston
    School Department, Cranston
South Carolina: Bill Chaiken, Anderson School District #5, Anderson; Karen
    Callison, Greenwood County School District #50, Greenwood; Ed White, Apple
    Computers, Spartanburg
South Dakota: J. D. Myers, Watertown Senior High Schools, Watertown; Virginia
    Tobin, Aberdeen Public Schools, Aberdeen
Tennessee: Robert Roney, University of Tennessee, Knoxville; Margaret Phelps,
    Tennessee Tech University, Cookeville; Cindy Chance, Milan City Schools, Milan
Texas: Genevieve Mandina, Sam Houston State University, Huntsville; Robert
    Coleman, Educational Service Center, Waco; Carol Kuykendal, Public Schools,

Houston; Barbara Wagner, University of Texas, Tyler; LeRoy Psencik, Texas Education Association, Austin; Charles Patterson, Kaleen Independent School District, Kaleen

Utah: Corrine Hill, Public Schools, Salt Lake City; Allan R. Nelson, Jordan School District, Sandy

Vermont: Charles Ginnett, Orleans Elementary School, Orleans; George Fuller, Orleans Central School District, Orleans

Virginia: Delores Greene, City Schools, Richmond; Evelyn Bickham, Lynchburg College, Lynchburg; Marion Hargrove, Public Schools, Redford; Shelba Murphy, EDIT, Inc., Alexandria

Virgin Islands: Mavis Brady, State Department of Education, St. Thomas

Washington: Richard Harris, Public Schools, Tacoma; Joe Fleming, Education Service District #114, Port Townsend; Monica Schmidt, State Board of Education, Olympia

West Virginia: Barbara Divins, Fairmont State College, Fairmont; Helen Saunders, State Department of Education, Charleston

Wisconsin: Carlyle Button, Gebhardt Elementary School, Black River Falls; John J. Koehn, Oconomowoc Public Schools, Oconomowoc; Arnold Chandler, Department of Public Instruction, Madison

Wyoming: Peter C. Ellsworth, University of Wyoming, Laramie; Donna Conner, University of Wyoming, Rawlins

International Units:

Canada: Jan Sarkissian, Victoria School District

Germany: Myrna Berg, Hainerberg Elementary School

United Kingdom: Richard Strickland, Department of Defense Dependents Schools

ASCD Review Council

Chair: Gerald Firth, University of Georgia, Athens
Barbara D. Day, University of North Carolina, Chapel Hill
J. Arch Phillips, Kent State University, Kent, Ohio
Elizabeth S. Randolph (retired), Charlotte-Mecklenburg Schools, Charlotte, North
   Carolina

ASCD Headquarters Staff

Gordon Cawelti, *Executive Director*
Ronald S. Brandt, *Executive Editor*
Jean Hall, *Associate Director*
Diane G. Berreth, *Associate Director*
Lewis A. Rhodes, *Assistant Director*
Jan Adkisson, *Acting Assistant Director*
John Bralove, *Business Manager*

Staff Members:

Samantha Anderson
Sarah Arlington
Nicky Atwood
Joan Brandt
Rene Brown
Raiza Chernault
Sandra Claxton
Nancy Condon
Marcia D'Arcangelo
Pamela Dronka
Elaine Dull
Anita Fitzpatrick
Susan Frank
Cerylle Fritts
Charles Green
Jim Green
Mary Hines
Jo Ann Irick
Deborah Johnson
Teola Jones

Rita Kefalas
Andre Keith
Leslie Ling
Josefa Manlapaz
Debbie Maddox
Clara Meredith
Frances Mindel
Nancy Modrak
Mavis Payton
Merrie Jo Perkuchin
Gayle Rockwell
Fran Schweiger
Robert Shannon
Carolyn Shell
Lisa Street
Dee Stump-Walek
Cindy Titus
Liz Trexler
Al Way
Colette Williams